613.7 Antonacci, Robert J.
ANT
Physical fitness for
young champions

DATE		
DE 6 '85		
MY 29 '87		
FEB 05 '93		

Physical Fitness for Young Champions
Second Edition

Physical Fitness
For Young Champions

Second Edition

Robert J. Antonacci
and Jene Barr
illustrated by Frank Mullins

McGraw-Hill Book Company

New York   St. Louis   San Francisco   Auckland   Düsseldorf
Johannesburg   Kuala Lumpur   London   Mexico   Montreal
New Delhi   Panama   Paris   São Paulo   Singapore   Sydney
Tokyo   Toronto

Also by Robert J. Antonacci and Jene Barr
BASEBALL FOR YOUNG CHAMPIONS
FOOTBALL FOR YOUNG CHAMPIONS
BASKETBALL FOR YOUNG CHAMPIONS

Robert J. Antonacci is a coauthor of
SPORTS OFFICIATING
TRACK AND FIELD FOR YOUNG CHAMPIONS

Jene Barr is author of
THIS IS MY COUNTRY
DAN THE WEATHERMAN
GOOD MORNING, TEACHER
and others

Library of Congress Cataloging in Publication Data

Antonacci, Robert Joseph, date
    Physical fitness for young champions.

    Includes index.
    SUMMARY: Examines requirements for physical fitness;
describes exercises to develop muscle strength, coordination, and speed; and suggests activities for keeping
fit.
    1. Physical education for children—Juvenile liter-
ature. [1. Physical fitness. 2. Exercise] I. Barr,
Jene, joint author. II. Mullins, Frank, ill. III. Ti-
tle.
GV443.A536   1975   613.7′042   75-2226
ISBN 0-07-002142-2 lib. bdg.

4567 BPBP 789876

Contents

CHAPTER 1

Your Physical Fitness IQ

On your mark! Get Set! Go! The Olympic runners are off! With long quick strides they tear along the turf. Number Four sprints into the lead. With the smoothness of a well-oiled machine he races with power-filled strides. The other runners are close at his heels. Just ahead stretches the finish line. Like a refueled engine Number Four bursts ahead. The distance between him and the other runners widens. With a tremendous spurt he dashes against the tape! Another Olympic record is broken!

Lift off! The gleaming space capsule trembles. Inside the capsule the astronaut hears the roar of the booster engine. As the space vehicle is borne away from the earth, all systems are "Go." The astronaut is physically fit and ready for the important work he must do.

These are two special examples of trained persons to whom the highest degree of physical fitness is essential.

But what about those of us who watch their feats—perhaps as we sit in front of our television sets? We live in a time of increasing automation. We no longer chop wood, as our ancestors did, or carry pails of water to the house, or hike miles to school. How fit are we for our part in this space age?

There is a saying: "A nation is as good as the people in it." This means that a country is in good condition when its people are fit—socially, emotionally, intellectually fit, and also *physically fit.*

Because physical fitness is so important, the President of the United States has asked all the people to help our country by keeping strong and healthy and active. He often calls together a Council on Physical Fitness and Sports to study our physical fitness and to urge all Americans to do daily exercises to improve our health so that we may work and look and feel better.

The Council on Physical Fitness and Sports is made up of the President himself, some special advisors, professional consultants, and other citizens who are interested in physical fitness and sports. There are several questions this council would like to ask you.

Do you practice warm-up exercises every day? Do you walk and hike and climb? Do you play on a team? Do you help with work around the house? How active are you? How physically fit are you?

How physically fit are you? The special tests in this book will help you rate yourself. How can you strengthen your weak points? The exercises and games which are described will help you. You will want to try them alone and with friends. But first of all, just what is complete physical fitness?

Complete Physical Fitness

There are ten general requirements for complete physical fitness. These are so important that you may want to list them in a Physical Fitness Notebook and begin to rate yourself as you read about each one.

1. The ability to fight or ward off illness.
2. A sound heart and healthy breathing system.
3. Muscles that have strength.
4. Muscles that have "explosive power."
5. Ability to move with speed.
6. Body agility.
7. Ability to move with accuracy.
8. Flexible muscles and joints.
9. Body balance.
10. Coordination of body movements.

Let us take each of these requirements and see what they mean and how we measure up to complete physical fitness.

Doctor's Check-Up

CAN YOU FIGHT ILLNESS?   Are you able to keep well or do you get sick easily? Do you complain of aches and pains often?

If you are able to keep from getting sick, hold onto your good health by following these rules:
1. Eat good nourishing meals.
2. Keep your body clean. Brush your teeth and bathe often.
3. Take care of cuts and bruises immediately.

4. Get enough rest, sleep, and relaxation.
5. Young athletes and champions do not smoke.
6. Wear clothes that fit well and dress properly for hot, cold, and rainy weather.
7. Get plenty of fresh air.
8. Be active! Play games and take plenty of exercise.

Obey these simple health rules, and sickness will have a hard time catching up with you.

But if you *do* get sick often, visit your doctor for a complete physical examination and then follow the doctor's orders.

Stamina and Endurance

FOR A HEALTHY HEART. Can you work and play hard without having to "fight for air?" Do you find it hard to breathe even during a short workout? Your *heart* and *breathing organs* are practically the "heart" of physical fitness. No matter how strong your muscles may be, you cannot put much strain on them unless your heart and breathing machinery have plenty of endurance.

Walk! Run! Work! Play games! These are just a few ways to build a strong, healthy heart and improve the endurance of your breathing system.

Remember this fact: The heart is a muscle and you cannot improve it without taking part in vigorous exercises and games.

How Strong Are Your Muscles? Can you work and play vigorously without having your muscles get tired too quickly?

You need strength in your arm and shoulder muscles to handle a baseball bat, swing a tennis racket, swim. It takes *muscle strength* to climb, to carry groceries, books, and other heavy things. It even takes strength to sit correctly at your desk in school!

To improve your muscle strength, do warm-ups and calisthenics every day. And play games.

For Stronger Muscles

For Those Rocket Jumps! Do you have springy action in your legs like the rabbit and kangaroo? They move with "explosive power." The basketball champion, broad jumper, and high jumper have this explosive power in their muscles, too.

You can improve the explosive power in your legs by practicing the standing and running broad jumps and the high jump. Also try the rocket jumps. Just jump higher and higher with every jump!

11

In everyday life you need this *explosive power* for many things—for example, to keep from bumping into teammates when playing games, perhaps even to jump out of the path of an oncoming bicycle or car.

Explosive Power Jumps

MOVE WITH MORE SPEED.   You need speed for many things ranging from a game of "tag" to running the bases in baseball. How fast do your legs move in the 50-yard dash? Can you sprint across a football field for a touchdown? Across the basketball court to guard a speedy opponent?

12

Speed Running

Speed is the rate at which you move. Can you move as fast as your friends?

You can improve your *speed* by doing short sprints, chasing fly balls, and running races.

ARE YOU NIMBLE? Can you run, dodge, pivot, and twist? You need these skills for the movements you make every day.

A champion ball-carrier knows how to slow down on a run. He knows how to put on the speed. He can

Agile Dodging

run in different directions. This is *agility of movement*!

You need this agility in basketball for dribble plays, in football when you fake a pass, or in baseball when you are caught between the bases.

Learn to be nimble by practicing these exercises: Run for short distances, forward, backward, and in zigzag directions. Run and stop and run and stop in different directions, over and over again. The games of tag and dodge ball are also fine agility exercisers.

Bowl for a Strike

CAN YOU HIT THE BULL'S EYE? Can you throw or kick to a certain spot? Can you make a basketball sink into the basket? Kick a football over the goal post? Pitch a strike over the heart of the plate? That's what the champions do all the time. This is known as control and *accuracy*!

You need this accuracy for sports. For the work you do in and out of school. When you work on hobbies.

Accuracy takes a great deal of practice. Athletes spend much time trying to improve their accuracy.

Set up some targets, and practice alone or with your friends. Throw and catch a baseball, football, and volleyball. But don't forget your daily workouts!

LIMBER UP! You need flexible muscles and joints for bending and stretching and twisting.

Figure skaters, swimmers, and tumblers have flexible muscles and joints. It's this flexibility that helps football and basketball champions twist and dodge away for winning plays.

Stretch for Flexibility

You can improve your *flexibility* by training your muscles. Limber up with daily exercises. Touch your toes without bending your knees. Do arm and shoulder movements. Sit-ups and leg raising.

HOW'S YOUR BODY BALANCE? Do you trip or fall easily? Without a sense of balance, you would not be able to stand or run or jump. Good body balance means that the muscles work well together just as a team works together.

It's this kind of balance that you need when you do a handstand or figure skating. And to keep from falling after you jump for a high pass.

Exercises can help you improve your *body balance.* Stand in one spot with your eyes closed. Now do this same thing with one leg raised. Walk along on a straight line or on a balance beam.

How Smooth Are Your Movements? A top athlete moves with smoothness. His smooth motions are a combination of muscle strength, body balance, speed, and agility. This is body *coordination.*

A big-league pitcher has this smoothness from the moment he winds up to the end of the throw and follow-through. You need this muscle coordination when you bat a ball, catch a pass, kick a football, or toss for a basket.

Improve your coordination by practicing the movements you need. Work on each movement over and over again until you get the "feel" of smoothness.

True Balance

Smooth Pitching

How Do You Measure Up?

If you wrote these ten requirements for complete physical fitness in your Fitness Notebook, check each carefully and answer this question: How well do I measure up? Then get to work and try to improve in those areas where you are weak.

CHAPTER 2

Can You Pass These Tests?

You take many kinds of tests from the time you are young until you become quite old. In school, your teachers give tests to find out how well you understand your subjects. You go to your doctor for a checkup or health test. Your gym teacher gives physical fitness tests.

Physical Fitness Tests

There are many kinds of physical fitness tests. The astronauts must pass a very rigid test before they can be accepted.

In the army, navy, and air-force academies, the cadets must pass fitness tests before they enter, while they are there, and before they graduate to become officers.

Boy Scouts, Girl Scouts, and other organizations give fitness tests to boys and girls. There are also physical fitness tests for men and women.

KRAUS-WEBER TEST. Let's take a test right now to see if you can do some simple exercises. This test will measure your *minimum muscle fitness*. It is known as the Kraus-Weber Test. It was developed by Dr. Hans Kraus and Dr. Sonja Weber. They are well-known doctors who do a great deal of work in physical fitness with hospital patients as well as with healthy people.

Dr. Kraus and Dr. Weber made up this test to measure the least possible amount of fitness a healthy person should have. You should be able to do *more* than this test calls for.

Rules for Kraus-Weber Test
1. Do each exercise only *once*.
2. Go from one exercise to the next *without stopping*. Let's begin!

Exercise 1. Lie on your back. Place both hands behind your neck. Keep your legs straight and have a partner hold your ankles firmly in place.

Roll up to a sitting position. Do not keep your back stiff or straight in this exercise.

Exercise 2. Lie on your back with hands behind your neck. Bend both knees close to your body, keeping your feet flat on the floor. Have a partner hold your feet down firmly. *Roll up* to a sitting position.

Exercise 3. Lie on your back with hands behind your neck. Keep knees straight and raise both legs so that your heels are 10 inches from the floor. Hold this position for ten seconds. Lower your legs.

Exercise 4. Lie face downward and place a rolled-up pillow or blanket under your hips. Place both hands behind your neck. Have a partner place one hand upon your ankles and his other hand over the lower part of your back. Raise your chest from the floor and hold this position for ten seconds.

Exercise 5. Lie face downward with a rolled pillow under your hips. Have a partner place one hand over your shoulders and his other hand upon the lower part of your back.

Raise your legs off the floor, keeping your knees straight. Hold this position for ten seconds.

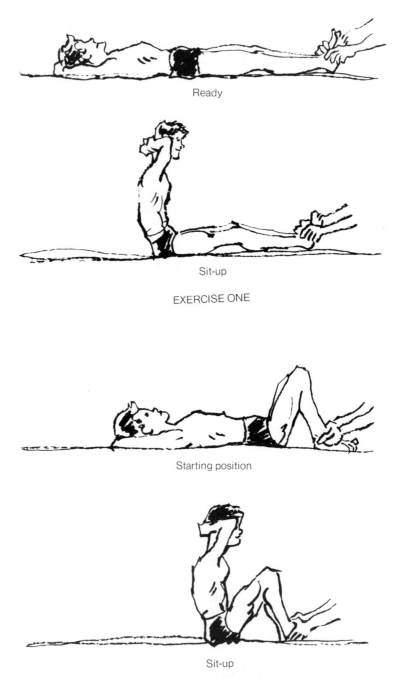

Ready

Sit-up

EXERCISE ONE

Starting position

Sit-up

EXERCISE TWO

20

Exercise 6. Stand erect with feet together and knees straight. Bend down and touch toes with your finger-tips. Do not bounce or bob as you try to touch your toes.

Fair Condition. If you passed all six exercises in the Kraus-Weber Test it means that you are able to meet the *least possible requirements* for physical fitness.

This test pointed out the condition of your muscles in the back and hip area. It also told whether your trunk muscles were flexible. If you cannot do any exercises harder than these your body is in only *fair* condition.

And just think! This test *did not* measure your body endurance, coordination, agility, strength, speed, or explosive muscle power. But there's another test that will let you know how well you can do in these areas.

YOUTH PHYSICAL FITNESS TEST. The President's Council prepared a test which will show how fit and active you are. It is known as the Youth Physical Fitness Test. This test has been given to millions of boys and girls in the United States to measure their physical fitness.

Rules for Taking Youth Physical Fitness Test
1. This test is for boys and girls from ten to seventeen years of age.
2. You may take this test indoors or out-of-doors.
3. If you are under ten years of age *do not try* to see how many times you can do each exercise. (But you may use these exercises for practice and to get in condition.)
4. If you are ten to seventeen years of age try to reach the *Presidential or excellent mark.*
5. Take a short warm-up before beginning the test.
6. If possible, divide the test into two parts. Take the first part on one day and the second part on the next day.

Hold—10 seconds

EXERCISE THREE

Hold—10 seconds

EXERCISE FOUR

Hold—10 seconds

EXERCISE FIVE

22

Touch your toes

EXERCISE SIX

FIRST DAY	SECOND DAY
pull-ups	50-yard dash
sit-ups	softball throw
standing broad jump	600-yard run-and-walk
shuttle run	

HOW WILL YOU RATE? If you are overweight you may have a hard time chinning or doing pull-ups. If you are underweight, sit-ups may be hard to do. This means that you should watch your eating habits. Also, you may need to be more active in your spare time.

The way you rate in this test will help you find out your strong and weak points. If you show weakness in some places, work to improve. But if you are strong and make a good rating, hold on to your strength by keeping up with your exercises and games.

AWARDS FROM THE PRESIDENT. Every boy and girl is eligible to earn a special award from the President of the United States. You may choose to earn a *certificate* signed by the President, which can be framed and hung on your favorite wall. Or, you may wish a special *badge* or *emblem* that can be worn on a jacket or

23

sweater. To earn one of these awards you must reach the *Presidential Award* or *excellent* mark that's recorded for each of the seven exercise tests of the Youth Physical Fitness Test. Your teacher or any adult working for a youth organization must sign your official form supplied by the President's Council on Physical Fitness and Sports. If you are under ten years of age, keep using these exercises for practice and conditioning. This will get you ready when it becomes your turn to qualify for an award.

Youth Physical Fitness Test: First Day

Pull-ups (Boys)
This test measures your arm and shoulder strength.

a. Grasp the chinning bar with both hands, palms facing forward.
b. Hang with arms and legs straight. Feet should not touch the floor.
c. Bend your arms and pull yourself up until your chin reaches over the bar. Do not raise your knees or kick or swing as you pull yourself up.
d. Lower your body until your arms are straight. Repeat this exercise as many times as you can. Come to a complete hang position between each pull-up.

PULL-UPS SCORE FOR BOYS

Rating	Age—10	11	12	13	14	15	16	17
Excellent	8	8	9	10	12	13	14	16
Presidential Award	6	6	6	8	10	10	12	12
Good	5	5	5	7	8	10	11	12
Satisfactory	3	3	3	4	6	7	9	9
Poor	1	1	1	2	4	5	6	7

Ready   Pull up and down

EXERCISE ONE

Key to Score: Your rating is based on your age and the number of times you completed the exercise.

Age: Find your age in the top row.

Number of pull-ups: Locate the number of pull-ups you completed in the column below your age.

Rating: Check the number of pull-ups you did and find your rating in the left-hand column.

Example: If you are ten years old and completed eight pull-ups your rating is *excellent*.

If you are ten years old and completed six pull-ups your rating is at *Presidential Award* level. If you did five pull-ups your rating is *good*. If you did three or four pull-ups, your rating remains *satisfactory* but it is closer to the good mark.

Pull-ups, Bent-arm Hang (Girls)

Girls' pull-ups are done in a somewhat different way.

25

The chinning bar must be lowered to standing height.

a. Stand close to the bar with your feet slightly apart and barely touching the ground.

b. Grasp the bar with both hands, palms facing forward.

c. Bend (flex) your arms and pull yourself up so that your chin is just above the bar, with elbows bent and chest close to the bar (one or two partners may help raise you upward to this position).

Ready   Pull up

Extra Practice Pull-ups

d. Feet are off the ground. Hold this position. No help.

e. Now, have a partner check you to see *how long you can hold the same position* with any watch that can mark the seconds.

f. Partner stops timing when 1) chin touches bar, 2) head moves back to keep chin above bar, 3) chin drops below the bar. Knee raising and leg kicking is not permitted.

g. Total the number of seconds you held the same
    position. Look up your rating for your age on the
    chart for the Girls' Pull-ups.

Ready

EXERCISE ONE

Pull up and "hold"

PULL-UPS, BENT-ARM HANG SCORE FOR GIRLS

Rating	Age—10	11	12	13	14	15	16	17
			Time in Seconds					
Excellent	31	35	30	30	30	33	37	31
Presidential Award	21	20	19	18	19	18	19	19
Good	18	17	15	16	16	16	16	16
Satisfactory	10	10	8	9	9	10	9	10
Poor	6	5	5	5	5	6	5	6

Sit-ups (Boys and Girls)

This exercise measures the strength in the stomach
muscles and the condition of the hip joints.

a. Lie on your back with fingers of both hands laced
    behind your head. Have a partner hold your ankles
    firmly in place, knees slightly up.

27

b. Raise your trunk to a sit-up position.
c. Turn your trunk to the left and touch your left knee with your right elbow.
d. Return to a lying position.
e. Again sit up, turn your trunk to the right, and touch your right knee with your left elbow. Every time you touch your knee with the elbow, it is one complete sit-up.
Repeat, touching left knee, right knee, as many times as you can.

SIT-UPS SCORE FOR BOYS

Rating	Age—10	11	12	13	14	15	16	17
Excellent	100	100	100	100	100	100	100	100
Presidential Award	100	100	100	100	100	100	100	100
Good	76	89	100	100	100	100	100	100
Satisfactory	50	50	59	75	99	99	99	85
Poor	34	35	42	50	60	61	63	57

SIT-UPS SCORE FOR GIRLS

Rating	Age—10	11	12	13	14	15	16	17
Excellent	50	50	50	50	50	50	50	50
Presidential Award	50	50	50	50	50	50	50	50
Good	50	50	50	50	49	42	41	45
Satisfactory	39	37	39	38	34	30	30	30
Poor	26	26	26	27	25	24	24	23

Standing Broad Jump (Boys and Girls)
This test will measure the explosive power in your leg muscles.
a. Take a position just behind the take-off line, with your feet from 6 to 10 inches apart (whatever is most comfortable).

b. Bend your knees and swing your arms back and forth with an even motion.

c. Lean a trifle forward, swing arms swiftly forward and upward and take off from the balls of your feet with an explosive spring through the air.

Measure the distance from the take-off line to the spot where your heels or any other part of your body landed nearest the take-off line.

Repeat this exercise three times and measure each jump.

Write down the mark of your best jump in feet and inches for your score.

Ready

Explosive jump

EXERCISE THREE

Land

STANDING BROAD JUMP (BOYS)

Rating	Age—10	11	12	13	14	15	16	17
				Feet-Inches				
Excellent	6-1	6-3	6-6	7-2	7-9	8-0	8-5	8-6
Presidential Award	5-8	5-10	6-2	6-9	7-3	7-6	7-11	8-1
Good	5-7	5-9	6-1	6-7	7-0	7-6	7-9	8-0
Satisfactory	5-2	5-4	5-8	6-0	6-7	6-0	7-4	7-6
Poor	4-10	5-0	5-4	5-7	6-1	6-6	6-11	7-0

Key: This jump is measured in feet and inches. The first number shows the feet and the second number, the inches.

Example: 6-1 is 6 feet and 1 inch.

STANDING BROAD JUMP (GIRLS)

Rating	Age—10	11	12	13	14	15	16	17
				Feet-Inches				
Excellent	5-8	6-2	6-3	6-3	6-4	6-6	6-7	6-8
Presidential Award	5-4	5-8	5-9	5-10	6-0	6-1	6-2	6-2
Good	5-2	5-6	5-8	5-8	5-10	6-0	6-0	6-0
Satisfactory	4-10	5-0	5-2	5-3	5-5	5-6	5-6	5-7
Poor	4-5	4-8	4-9	4-10	5-0	5-1	5-2	5-2

Shuttle Run (Boys and Girls)

This test will measure your body agility and flexibility of the hip joints.

Mark two parallel lines 30 feet apart. Place two wooden blocks (about the size of blackboard erasers) just behind the far line. Have a partner check your running time with a stopwatch or any watch that can mark the seconds and tenths of seconds.

a. Take a running stance behind the starting line.

b. On the signal, "Ready—Go!" run swiftly toward the blocks. Pick one up, race back, and set the block behind the starting line.

c. Without stopping, run for the other block, pick it up, and speed back across the starting line without stopping to put this second block down.
Take two trials in this test. Mark down the time for your fastest run as your score.

SHUTTLE RUN (BOYS)

Rating	Age—10	11	12	13	14	15	16	17
	Time in seconds and tenths of a second							
Excellent	10.0	10.0	9.8	9.5	9.3	9.1	9.0	8.9
Presidential Award	10.4	10.3	10.0	9.9	9.6	9.4	9.2	9.1
Good	10.5	10.4	10.2	10.0	9.8	9.5	9.3	9.2
Satisfactory	11.0	10.9	10.7	10.4	10.0	9.8	9.7	9.6
Poor	11.5	11.3	11.1	10.9	10.5	10.1	10.0	10.0

Pick up, turn, and run

EXERCISE FOUR

Key to measure running time: The number to the left of the decimal point is *seconds.* The number to the right of the decimal is *tenths of a second.*

Example: If you are eleven years old and ran the race for a score of good, your time was *ten and four-tenths seconds.*

SHUTTLE RUN (GIRLS)

Rating	Age—10	11	12	13	14	15	16	17
	Time in seconds and tenths of a second							
Excellent	10.0	10.0	10.0	10.0	10.0	10.0	10.0	10.0
Presidential Award	10.8	10.6	10.5	10.5	10.4	10.5	10.4	10.4
Good	11.0	10.9	10.8	10.6	10.5	10.7	10.6	10.5
Satisfactory	11.5	11.4	11.3	11.1	11.0	11.1	11.0	11.0
Poor	12.0	12.0	11.9	11.8	11.5	11.6	11.5	11.5

Tests for the Second Day

50-yard Dash (Boys and Girls)

This test measures your speed in running.

Mark a starting line and a finish line 50 yards apart. The starter, with a timing watch in his hand, stands at the finish line.

a. Take a sprinter's position behind the starting line.
b. When the starter raises his hand, this is the signal to "Get Ready!"
c. When he brings his hand down "Go!" Run as fast as you can across the finish line.

50-YARD DASH (BOYS)

Rating	Age—10	11	12	13	14	15	16	17
	Time in seconds and tenths of a second							
Excellent	7.0	7.0	6.8	6.5	6.3	6.1	6.0	6.0
Presidential Award	7.4	7.4	7.0	6.9	6.6	6.4	6.2	6.1
Good	7.5	7.5	7.2	7.0	6.7	6.5	6.3	6.2
Satisfactory	8.0	7.8	7.6	7.3	7.0	6.7	6.5	6.5
Poor	8.5	8.1	8.0	7.6	7.2	7.0	6.8	6.7

Key: Running time is measured in seconds and tenths of seconds.

Example: If you are eleven years old and ran the 50-yard dash in 7.4, it means seven and four-tenths seconds.

50-YARD DASH (GIRLS)

Rating	Age—10	11	12	13	14	15	16	17
	Time in seconds and tenths of a second							
Excellent	7.0	7.0	7.0	7.0	7.0	7.1	7.0	7.1
Presidential Award	7.5	7.6	7.5	7.5	7.4	7.5	7.5	7.5
Good	7.7	7.7	7.6	7.6	7.5	7.6	7.5	7.6
Satisfactory	8.2	8.1	8.0	8.0	7.9	8.0	8.0	8.0
Poor	8.8	8.5	8.4	8.4	8.3	8.3	8.5	8.5

Softball Throw for Distance (Boys and Girls)

This test measures body coordination and the explosive power in your throwing arm.

You can take this test on an open field, playground, or football or baseball field. Use a 12-inch softball. Mark a starting line. Have a partner measure the throw with a tape measure.

a. Take an outfielder's throwing position about 6 to 10 feet behind the starting line.

b. Start your windup and begin moving forward at the same time.

c. Get as close as possible to the starting line and throw the ball overhand as far as you can. *Do not step over* the starting line or it will be a foul.

Your partner will place a stake to mark the spot where the ball hit the ground first. You are allowed to have three tries and the best one is set down as your score.

THROW FOR DISTANCE (BOYS)

Rating	Age—10	11	12	13	14	15	16	17
				Feet				
Excellent	138	151	165	185	208	221	238	249
Presidential Award	122	136	150	175	187	204	213	226
Good	118	129	145	168	181	198	207	218
Satisfactory	102	115	129	147	165	180	189	198
Poor	91	105	115	131	146	165	172	180

Key: The throw for distance is measured in *feet* from the take-off line to the spot where it lands first. The numbers on the chart show the number of feet the ball should travel for each age.

THROW FOR DISTANCE (GIRLS)

Rating	Age—10	11	12	13	14	15	16	17
				Feet				
Excellent	84	95	103	111	114	120	123	120
Presidential Award	71	81	90	94	100	105	104	102
Good	69	77	85	90	95	100	98	98
Satisfactory	54	64	70	75	80	84	81	82
Poor	46	55	59	65	70	73	71	71

600-yard Run-Walk

This test will tell whether you have good heart and breathing endurance and will also measure the strength and endurance in your leg muscles.

Take this test on an open field, playground, running track, baseball or football field—whichever is available.

You do not have to run on a straight course. You can run around the bases of a baseball diamond or around a football field. Mark a starting line and a finish line 600 yards apart. A partner stands at the finish line with a timing watch.

a. Take a runner's position behind the starting line.

b. On the signal "Ready—Go!" take off and run! You can walk part of the way, but the idea is to cover the 600 yards as fast as you can.

600-YARD RUN-WALK (BOYS)

Rating	Age—10	11	12	13	14	15	16	17
			Time in minutes and seconds					
Excellent	1:58	1:59	1:52	1:46	1:37	1:34	1:32	1:31
Presidential Award	2:12	2:8	2:2	1:53	1:46	1:40	1:37	1:36

Good	2:15	2:11	2:5	1:55	1:48	1:42	1:39	1:38
Satisfactory	2:26	2:21	2:15	2:5	1:57	1:49	1:47	1:45
Poor	2:40	2:33	2:26	2:15	2:5	1:58	1:56	1:54

Key: The 600-yard run-walk is measured in minutes and seconds. The number at the left of the colon shows the minutes. The number on the right shows the seconds.

Example: If you are ten years old and finished this test in 2:12, it means that you covered the distance in two minutes and twelve seconds.

If you are twelve years old and scored 2:2, you covered the distance in two minutes and two seconds.

600-YARD RUN-WALK (GIRLS)

Rating Age—	*10*	*11*	*12*	*13*	*14*	*15*	*16*	*17*
	Time in minutes and seconds							
Excellent	2:5	2:13	2:14	2:12	2:9	2:9	2:10	2:11
Presidential Award	2:20	2:24	2:24	2:25	2:22	2:23	2:23	2:27
Good	2:26	2:28	2:27	2:29	2:25	2:26	2:26	2:31
Satisfactory	2:41	2:43	2:42	2:44	2:41	2:40	2:42	2:46
Poor	2:55	2:59	2:58	3:0	2:55	2:52	2:56	3:0

What Is Your Score?
Did you make a rating of excellent in all the exercises? If not, try answering these questions:
1. Do you use the right *sets of muscles* for the different movements throughout the body?
   Do you use these muscles often enough to develop and make them stronger?
2. Do you take part *steadily* in games and sports?
   Or do you let your muscles become flabby?
3. Do you watch your weight?
   If you are overweight or underweight you must watch the kind and amount of food you eat.

4. Do you feel well?
   If you "huff and puff" when you work or play you should go to your doctor for a health checkup.

For a Better Score

Any one of these reasons could be the cause for a poor showing on the Youth Fitness Test. This means that you should do a regular workout *every day*!

To make this workout more fun, choose some exercises that will help you feel better and play better in your favorite sport. Throw and catch a baseball, basketball, or football. Run and jump. Do some 25-yard runs. Then try the 50-yard runs. Do standing and running broad jumps. And don't neglect rope jumping. Keep your body *active* every single day!

Keep working at your fitness program and test yourself every three months. This is the way to improve.

HINT

When you *do* reach the mark of excellent for each part of the test, don't stop your workouts or you'll get soft again. Make that daily workout a "must!" That's the way to reach and hold onto a good score.

So, dig in! Follow the advice of the President's Council on Physical Fitness and Sports. Start on a plan of exercises to meet the requirements for physical fitness, if your doctor has found you in good health. Also be active and play games all year around. That's the way to build up your health and strength. And that's the way to help your country, too!

Now let's discuss some exercises which will help you.

CHAPTER 3

Exercises for Muscle Strength

How good was your rating on the Youth Fitness Test you have just taken? And what are your answers to the following questions?

When you go out on a hike or do a little work or play a game, do your shoulders sag? Do your muscles become stiff and tight? Are you able to swing that bat during a game? Are you able to carry a bundle of newspapers? Or groceries? Do you become weary with a little exertion? You may not have strength in your muscles.

If this is true, don't be discouraged. Here are exercises that can build up your muscles.

Arm and Shoulder Exercises

These exercises will help your muscles grow bigger and stronger.

PUSH-UPS. Lie on the floor, face down, with hands on the floor near your chest. Do some push-ups until your arm and shoulder muscles begin to get tired.

37

Starting position

Push up

PUSH-UPS

PULL-UPS (CHINS).   Stand close to a horizontal (chinning) bar that's at least 6 inches above your standing reach. With both hands shoulder-width apart, take a short jump and reach up and grasp the bar with an overhand grip.

Pull on the muscles until your chin touches over the bar but do not swing or kick your legs as you pull yourself up.

Straighten your arms slowly and lower your body. Work on this exercise without stopping until your arms become tired.

WALL PUSH-AWAY.   If the push-ups and pull-ups were hard to do, work on the following exercises to gain more strength.

Place both hands about shoulder-width apart against a wall. Bend your elbows and touch the wall with your chin, keeping your body straight. Straighten your arms and push away from the wall. Keep your feet firmly planted on the floor to prevent sliding.

SQUEEZE-BALL. Pitchers, boxers, and batters practice this exercise in their spare moments. It's a favorite with all the athletes who need a strong arm and grip.

Use a rubber or sponge ball. Squeeze the ball tightly over and over again, first with one hand and then with the other.

Roll and Unroll

WEIGHT ROLL-UP. With some cord tie or nail a 2-pound weight to a wooden stick so that the weight hangs about 3 feet below the stick.

Grip the stick at each end with your knuckles facing upward. Raise your arms to shoulder-height and turn the rod over and over in an outward direction until the weight is all rolled up. Then unroll slowly.

WEIGHT-LIFTING. Weight-lifting sets consist of long and short steel bars with weights of different sizes that can be attached to each end.

Short-Bar Drills

1. Grip a 2- to 5-pound bar with one hand and hold it close to your side. With a straight arm, knuckles facing upward, lift the weight forward to shoulder-height. Lower the weight to the starting position.
2. Grip a 5- to 10-pound bar with one hand and hold it close to your side. Bend your elbow and lift the

weight in front of you so that the bar touches your shoulder. Lower the weight to the starting position.

3. Lie on the floor or on a bench with a bar in one hand and both arms close to your body. Lift the bar upward with a straight arm and return slowly to the floor.

4. Repeat all these exercises with the other hand.

These weight-training exercises can also be done with a weight in each hand. As you improve, use

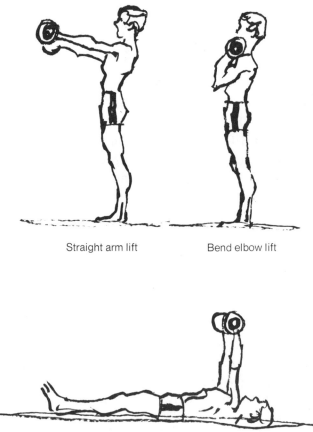

Straight arm lift   Bend elbow lift

Floor straight lift

TWO-ARM SHORT BAR DRILLS

heavier weights or repeat each drill with more speed.
If you don't have short-bar weights, use a book or small bundle of magazines in each hand.

Long-Bar Drills
1.Use a 10-pound weight for these long-bar drills.

1. Lifting position   2. Front rest

OVERHEAD PRESS

3. Bend elbow rest   4. Overhead press

With both hands grasp a long bar and repeat all the short-bar exercises.

2. Place the bar on the floor and stand directly behind the bar with your feet about shoulder-width apart. Bend knees to a squat position. Take an overhand grip on the bar. Look ahead. Keep your back and arms straight, slowly straighten your legs, and rest the bar against your body. *You have lifted the bar with the muscles in your legs!*

Bend your elbows and lift the bar so that it is close to your chin. Straighten your arms and lift the weight up over your head.

Bend your elbows and lower the weight in front of your body so it is close to your thighs.

Bend your knees to a squat position, keep your body straight, and set the weight on the ground. This is real weight-training!

You can also do this exercise by lowering the weight in back of your head.

WARNING
Do not try to see how heavy a weight you can lift. The important thing in these exercises is to give your muscles a workout.

HAND WRESTLING. Face a partner and plant your right foot against his right foot. Take your partner's right hand and hold it as though you were shaking hands.

Push or pull with your hand and try to force your partner to move his right foot. The one who forces the other to move away from his spot wins the game.

Try this exercise with a left-hand grip and with the left feet touching.

SOLO TUG-OF-WAR. Place the palms of both hands together and hook your fingers in a tight grip. Hold hands against your chest and raise your elbows shoulder-high.

Push both hands against each other for five seconds. Then pull with both hands for five seconds. Can you feel the chest, arm, and shoulder muscles working?

HEAD TUG-OF-WAR. This is especially good for the neck muscles.

Place the palm of your right hand against the right side of your neck. Push your hand against your head and your head against your hand at the same time for five seconds. Repeat with the left hand.

Now place both hands in back of your head and start your battle, hands pushing against your head.

Place your hands upon your forehead and play tug-of-war again. You should feel the pull of the muscles as you do all these drills.

SHOULDER SHRUGS. These exercises will stretch and relax the neck and shoulder muscles.
1. Let your arms hang loosely at your sides. Lift or shrug both shoulders upward as high as you can. Quickly lower your shoulders and stretch your neck upward.
2. Move shoulders forward and then push them back as far as they will go.
3. Try these shrug exercises with one shoulder at a time: up, down, forward, and backward.
4. Move shoulders around in a circle.

BENCH DIPS. Now you should be able to do these harder arm and shoulder exercises.

Place two low benches or footstools side by side about shoulder-width apart. Put one hand on each bench and stretch your legs toward the rear, keeping your body straight. Straighten your arms and push yourself up.

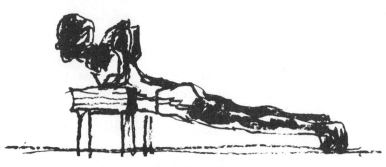

Dip and Push-Ups

Then bend your elbows and dip down as far as you can go between the two benches, keeping your body straight and rigid. See if you can do this "dip" exercise twice without stopping.

Parallel-Bar Exercises

1. *Bar Dips.* Take a firm grip over the top side of each bar and rest your elbows upon them. Push against the bars with both arms and lift your body until your arms are straight. Hold this position with head and chest up, and shoulders back.

Now "dip" down by bending your elbows, but do not rest your arms upon the bar. Can you push up once more from this position?

2. *Parallel-Bar Hand-Walk.* Take the same starting position. Lift yourself and straighten your arms. Shift the weight of your body toward the left, and slide your right hand a few inches forward.

Shift your weight toward the right, and slide your left hand a few inches forward. Keep shifting your weight from side to side and move each hand forward until you reach the end of the bars.

If you cannot do this hand-walk all the way, let go with both hands in front of your body and land on your feet.

44

Dip Down—Push up   Hand Walk along Bars

Back and Stomach Developers

Do you ever have a backache? Do you walk with a slouch? If so, your back and stomach muscles need some strengthening. These exercises should help you.

1. Seesaw Leg Lift

Lie flat on your stomach and place a small pillow under your hips. Fold your arms under your head and rest on them. Have a partner hold your shoulders down firmly.

With legs straight and feet together, lift your legs slowly off the floor and hold steady for ten seconds. Then lower legs to the floor.

2. Seesaw Back Lift

Take the same position as for the leg lift but fold both arms behind your neck. Have a partner hold your ankles down. Raise your chest slowly off the floor and hold this position for ten seconds. Lower chest to the floor.

To get a stronger pull on the muscles, try this exercise without a partner.

BEAT THE DRUM.   Lie on your back with legs spread about shoulder-width apart. Place one hand over each thigh.

Raise shoulders about 6 to 9 inches from the floor and move arms toward your knees. Lower your body to the starting position.

Hold—and Beat

Now raise your shoulders again and hold this position. Clench your hands and beat them gently upon your stomach muscles.

SIT-UPS.   Lie flat on your back with hands clasped under your neck and do some sit-ups until you feel your stomach muscles tire.

You can use a partner or put your feet under a couch or sofa.

SIT-UP AND TWIST.   Lie on the floor with legs spread and arms resting on your chest. Snap up quickly to a sitting position and touch your right toe with your left hand. Return to the starting position.

On the next sit-up, touch left toe with right hand.

Sit Up—Touch Toe

SNAP-UP "V." Lie on your back with hands resting on the floor near your head. With a quick snap-up, lift your legs and shoulders from the floor at the same time and try to touch your toes with both hands. Use a quick whipping motion of the arms to help you up. Come right back to the starting position.

Now for a harder one! Snap up quickly and hold this "V" position for five seconds.

Hold—5 Seconds

ROCKER. Lie on your stomach with arms stretched forward. Slowly raise your arms, chest, and legs from the floor; hold this position firmly and rock back and forth.

Another way to do this: Clasp your ankles in the "crab" position and rock back and forth on your stomach. You'll feel a good stretch in your muscles!

47

1. Stretch and Rock

2. "Crab" Rock

Leg Strength

Just think! Your legs carry the entire weight of your body wherever you want to go. So if you want to strengthen your leg muscles, get out and use them more often.

Rope Jumping

For a good leg conditioner get a rope and jump!
a. Jump and land on both feet.
b. Land on one foot at a time.
c. Jump with a high knee bend.
d. Jump and land in a squat position.

These are just a few kinds of jumps. Make up some rope-jumping exercises of your own and your leg muscles will get strong and muscular. Many athletes carry a jumping rope with them wherever they travel.

Knee Bend and One-half Squat

1. Stand straight with feet about shoulder-width apart and place your hands on your hips. Bend

knees to a one-half squat position, keeping your head, shoulders, and back straight. Return to the starting position.
2. Take the same starting position and bend one knee to a one-half squat. Straighten the other leg forward and raise it from the floor. Come back to the starting position on your standing leg. Try this exercise with the other leg.

You may need a chair to support yourself with one hand if this is hard to do at first.

LAZY MAN'S KICK. Sit well back on a chair or couch. Raise both legs and do the flutter-kick by raising one leg up as the other leg moves down. Keep legs straight and flutter-kick for ten seconds.

CHAIR LEG DIP. Stand, place both hands on back of chair and brace yourself against it. Bend your right knee slightly and stretch your left leg toward the rear and off the floor. Return to the starting position. Do the dip with the other leg.

As you can see, there are many exercises that will help your muscles grow bigger and stronger. Which of your muscles did you find weak or strong? Choose a few exercises to use in your daily workouts to strengthen your weak spots.

But you need more than muscle strength. You also need smoothness in all your movements. Let's try additional exercises that will help us achieve this smoothness and coordination.

CHAPTER 4

Exercises for Coordination

Can you twist and bend and stretch? Can you balance yourself and make accurate movements? Can you move smoothly? You need to make these movements for everyday living and especially for games and sports.

Limber Up for Flexible Muscles!

With stiff muscles and joints you cannot have much fun and you can injure yourself easily. So work on these bending and stretching exercises to limber up. Then you will be able to move with strength and smoothness.

ARM CIRCLES. Stand with feet together and raise your arms sideward to shoulder height with the palms facing upward.

Move both arms backwards in a 12-inch circle. You should be able to feel the stretch in your upper arm, chest, and shoulder muscles.

Raise arms upward and move them backward around in a 12-inch circle over your head. Keep your arms straight and put some zip into these circle drills.

DOUBLE PUNCH. Stand firmly with feet shoulder-width apart. Bend your arms, clench your hands, and push your elbows back. Punch forward swiftly with both fists and then drive your elbows back to the starting position.

Now, at the same time, drive your left fist over your right shoulder and the right fist over the left shoulder. Do this whole exercise in rhythm with strong, whipping movements: forward, back, across, back.

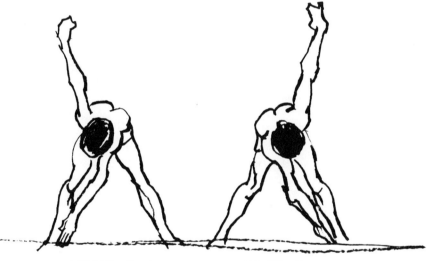

1. Right Toe Touch   2. Left Toe Touch

WINDMILL TWIST. Stand with feet spread wide apart and raise your arms sideward to shoulder level.

Bend trunk forward until your head is on a level with your hips. Do not bend knees. Twist your body and touch right toe with your left hand. At the same time, whip the right hand upward and back.

Twist your body in the opposite direction and touch left toe with your right hand. Repeat to the right and to the left with a strong, whipping motion.

You should feel a stretch in the muscles and joints.

1. Bob up and down   2. To knees   3. Down to toes

BOB AND SLAP!   Stand with feet shoulder-width apart and bend your trunk forward just a bit. Stretch arms toward the floor and make short "bobs" up and down with your hands sliding over your thighs. Keep bobbing lower and lower downward toward the ankles.

Now, without bobbing, bend forward and slap your thighs. Bend still lower and slap your knees. Keep bending and slap your toes! Keep knees straight all through this exercise.

LEG GRAPPLE.   Stand straight with your back touching a wall. Raise right leg as high as you can with the knee straight. Now bend the knee, clasp both arms under or around it and press the knee against your body. Do this exercise with the other leg.

STEP THROUGH HOOP.   Form a hoop by clasping both hands together in front of your body and bend forward. Lower your hands so that the hoop is knee-high.

Step into the hoop, first with one foot and then with the other, and do not break your hand grip. Your hands are now behind your back.

Now bend forward again and step out of the hoop with one leg at a time. For a greater challenge try this drill gripping a broomstick with hands about shoulder-width apart.

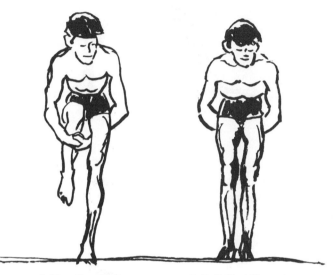

1. Step Over Hoop   2. Both Feet Through

SEESAW STRETCH. This exercise is good if you are overweight or have weak trunk muscles.

Stand with feet spread far apart. With palms facing downward raise your arms sideward to shoulder level. Bend trunk toward the right and place right hand on your thigh. Keep stretching right hand downward with short bobbing movements as far as you can go. At the same time, stretch your left hand up over your head. Face forward all through this exercise. Repeat this toward the left side.

Sideward Stretch—Down

RIDE A BICYCLE. Lie on your back, bend elbows, raise your legs, and rest your hips on your hands. Point your feet upward and pump up and down with your legs as though riding a bicycle.

Pedal Away

THE HURDLER. Sit on the floor with legs together. Slide the right leg around to the rear keeping knee bent and point the toes.

Stretch forward as far as possible and touch left toe with your left hand. Stretch your right arm toward the rear. You are now in the position of a hurdler. Bob forward a few times toward the front leg and keep that front leg straight.

Try this in the opposite direction, with the right foot forward and left leg toward the rear. You should feel a tremendous stretch in the muscles under the forward leg.

Hurdler

HEAD-ON-KNEE REST. Sit on the floor with legs spread. Bend toward the left leg and grasp the left ankle with your left hand. Place right hand under your left thigh.

With short bobbing movements bend until your head rests upon your left knee keeping leg straight. Repeat this toward the right side. You should feel a pull under the leg you are holding and on the opposite side in the back muscles.

MANY MORE FOR LIMBERING UP. Practice the football kick, ballet kick, and the forward, backward, and shoulder rolls.

From a standing and lying position, practice as many swimming strokes as you know. Try the solo elephant walk on all fours with hips high and legs and arms straight. These exercises should give you flexible joints and muscles.

Be Nimble!

You need nimbleness of movement in many things you do—when you make stop-and-go movements or when you must twist and dodge. Use a few *agility* drills every day with your workout.

HIGH KNEE RUNS. Bend your elbows and keep the arms close to your side. Run in place slowly for 5 seconds using a low knee action and an even leg movement. Pump the arms back and forth.

Now speed up with high knee action for 5 seconds. Then sprint forward for a few yards, toward the right, left and backward.

SHUTTLE RUN. Place two markers on the ground about 6 inches apart and 10 yards from a starting line.

Stand in back of the starting line and run toward the markers. Pick one up, run back, and place it on the starting line. Without stopping, go after the second marker and bring it back. This is *change-of-pace* running.

CAUGHT BETWEEN BASES. Place two flat markers on the ground about 50 feet apart. Stand between the markers as though you were a base runner caught between two bases.

Crouch slightly with feet spread and run with short, choppy steps toward one base and back again toward the other. Then make a quick sprint and pretend to slide into a base. This kind of *agility* helps win ball games.

THE SPRINTER. Place your hands on the ground about shoulder-width apart with arms straight. Set the left foot, knee bent, about 12 inches behind your hands. Push right leg farther back so that it is almost straight. Keep your head up and look straight ahead.

Sprinter

Rest weight on your hands and with a little upward thrust of the body, change the position of your legs quickly. Keep elbows straight and arms in the same place as you change your leg position.

Do this drill in rhythm: Left foot forward, right leg back and right foot forward, left leg back.

TIGER IN CIRCLE. Draw a circle about 10 feet in diameter. One player will be the "tiger" and stand in the center.

Two players stand outside the circle opposite each other. They move about the circle and toss a basketball back and forth to one another. The tiger tries to block or steal the passes. Each player should have a chance to be the tiger. Teams throughout the country use this sports drill.

57

FOR MORE AGILITY. For more practice in dodging, twisting, stopping, pivoting and short jumping, play "I've Got It," dodge ball, and tag. Also work on the movements a skier uses to make a quick turn. The movements a football player uses as he dodges and twists. The movements of a basketball player as he dribbles and pivots.

Lift Up for Body Balance!

When you trip over a chair you need body balance to stay on your feet. When you jump up to catch a ball you need body balance to land without falling over. Without a good sense of balance you are apt to fall easily at the slightest push when you work or play.

Hold—5 Seconds

Simple Balance Drills
1. Stand with feet together for ten seconds.
2. In the same position, close your eyes and stand still for ten seconds.

3. Take the same position, close your eyes, and raise one leg a few inches from the floor. Do all these drills without moving.

BALLET DRILL. Raise your arms forward or sideward to shoulder-height and lean forward so that your head and shoulders are about waist-high. Raise one leg toward the rear until it is level with your head and shoulders. Hold this position for five seconds. Try it with the other leg. If you need help, use a chair or wall for support.

TIGHTROPE WALK. Draw a line on the floor. Or use a line between two floor boards. Walk forward, step by step, along the line for 10 yards. Walk backward on the line.

BOOK BALANCE. Place a book upon your head. With hands on hips walk forward 10 feet. Bend one knee and raise the other leg forward and hold this position for five seconds. How did you do?

Board Walk

Board Walk.   Use a balance beam or board at least 4 inches wide. Step up on the board, keep your body erect, and walk forward. Stand sideways and sidestep toward the right and then toward the left. Now walk backward on the board. Use your arms as balancers.

1. Starting Position

2. Hold—5 Seconds

Frog Stand.   Take a squat position with hands on the floor and elbows pressed against the inside part of your knees. Lean forward a trifle, continue to press your elbows against your knees and put your weight upon your hands, keeping your head up. Slowly lift your feet a few inches off the ground and balance yourself for five seconds. Pretty tough, isn't it?

Wall Handstand.   Take the sprinter's starting position with hands on the floor about a foot away from the wall. Raise hips as high as possible with arms straight and fingers pointed toward the wall.

Put your weight on your hands and kick your rear leg upward, letting the other leg follow quickly until both legs rest against the wall. Now push both feet slowly a few inches away from the wall and see if you can balance on your hands. Keep elbows straight. If you cannot hold your balance, push your feet from the wall, bend at the hips, and land gently on the floor with one foot at a time.

Hit the Bull's-Eye

In sports there are some movements that take plenty of accuracy and control.

Basketball:	free throws, goals, and passing.
Baseball:	throwing, pitching.
Football:	place kicking, punting, and passing.
Soccer:	kick passing and kicking for goals.
Volleyball:	passing and hand striking for points.
Bowling:	aiming for strikes and spares.
Target Games:	fly and bait casting, archery.

There are many drills to help you gain control so you can hit the bull's-eye in all these games.

Baseball Target Drills

1. Mark a target on a wall or fence. The target should be $1^1/_2$ feet wide, 3 feet high and about knee-level above the ground. Stand 30 feet away and throw a soft ball at the target. Keep moving farther away until you can hit the target from a distance of 45 feet.

   Use a partner acting as a catcher and try to hit into his glove.
2. Mark a target on the ground and stand about 70 feet away. Throw the ball toward the target. Keep moving back until you can throw from a distance of 100 feet or more.

Football Target Drills

1. On a wall draw a marker 3 feet square and 3 feet above the ground. Stand 30 feet away and throw a

football at the marker. Keep moving back until you can hit at 45 feet. Now throw the ball to a partner who is on the run.
2. Hang an old tire or hoop to a tree or on a crossbar 5 to 8 feet above the ground. Stand 25 feet away and throw a football through the hoop or see if you can hit any part of it. Keep moving back and throw from a greater distance.

    Give the hoop a slight swing and try to hit this moving target.
3. On a regular football field use the 10-yard lines as guide markers. Or draw a straight long line on any open field.

    Stand at one end of the line and punt a football. See how far and how close to the line you can make the ball land.
4. Use the same marker line. Place the ball on a tee, or have a partner hold it and try for a kickoff or place kick.
5. Do these same kicks with a soccer ball.

In the Basket!
1. Use a regular basketball hoop and practice free-throw shots.
2. Stand 15 feet away and shoot the basketball through the hoop using the two-hand chest, over-hand shot, and one-hand jump shot.
3. Try these shots from different positions on the court. Increase the distance and see if you can hit through the hoop from a spot behind the free-throw line.

Aim for Accuracy
a. Hit a golf or tennis ball toward a certain spot.
b. Practice casting with a rod and reel.
c. Try passing a puck or some other flat object with a hockey stick.

d. Practice horseshoe pitching and bowling.

These sports drills will help improve your control, and they are also fun to do.

Muscle Teamwork for Coordination

A good swimmer cuts smoothly through the water. Every muscle works together in perfect rhythm. There is strength and smoothness from the beginning to the end of every movement. This is coordination!

| 1. Ready | 2. Jump | 3. Feet spread—arms up | 4. Jump back |

JUMPING JACK

JUMPING JACK. Stand with arms at your sides, feet together. Swing your arms sideward-upward, jump up and clap hands overhead and land with feet spread apart, all in one movement. Jump up and come back to the starting position. Do this in rapid rhythm.

HAND-AND-FOOT TAP. Take a standing position. Jump high into the air and quickly tap your feet with your hands before landing.

If this is hard to do, just tap one foot. Then try it with the other foot. Land on the balls of your feet and get your balance.

1. Jump and Tap   2. Land

RUSSIAN DANCE. Place one hand on a stool or chair. Bend knees to a complete squat and sit on your heels. Straighten left leg forward, take a short hop upward, and change the position of your feet. When you can do this well, try it without holding onto the chair.

MORE COORDINATION DRILLS. Skipping rope is fine. So is punching a boxing speed bag. Throw or punt a football. Throw and bat a baseball. Kick the soccer ball. Dribble a basketball. Work out a plan in your Fitness Notebook and include a few coordination exercises every day in your regular workouts. It will pay off in smooth movements with fine control.

CHAPTER 5

Exercises for Power
and Speed

A rocket soars into space with great force, speed, and *explosive power*! A champion broad jumper springs through the air in much the same way.

Your muscles act as your explosive power. You need this explosive power to run faster, throw farther, stretch higher, and make quick take-offs for short sprints, running bases, basketball rebounds, and catching football passes.

Your Explosive Power

Power up your muscles with these explosive power drills.

ROCKET JUMP!   Stand with arms loosely at your sides and bend your knees slowly to a squat position. Yell, "Rocket!" and jump as high as you can—stretching your arms toward the sky. Try to explode higher on every jump just like a rocket.

HOP FOR DISTANCE. Stand with your toes directly behind the starting line. Raise one foot, swing your arms back slowly, and bend the standing knee a trifle. Lean forward and push off on the standing leg and explode for a far hop through the air. Land on the push-off leg.

1. Push off   2. Jump   3. Land on push-off leg

HOP FOR DISTANCE

HOP, STEP, AND JUMP. Stand behind the starting line and raise your left leg. Hop forward with the right foot, take a long step with the left foot, push off and jump as far as you can and land on both feet with the arms and body in a forward position. Do this whole exercise without stopping. Try the hop, step, and jump with a running start.

BROAD JUMPS. Stand behind the take-off line with feet slightly apart, and raise both arms to shoulder height. Take a windup by bending your knees to a near squat position, bring your arms down behind your body, lean a bit forward, and swing your arms back and forth a few times.

Now as you whip your arms forward, explode on the take-off and spring upward and forward as far as you can go. You can also do this broad jump with a running start.

Another good explosive power drill is high jumping from a standing or running start. But be sure to have a coach or other adult help you in the high jump.

HEEL LIFTS. Perhaps you need more power in your leg muscles. These exercises should help you.

Stand with feet shoulder-width apart. Raise your heels as high as you can and then lower to the ground.

Now place a 2- by 4-inch board on the ground or use a bundle of newspapers or magazines about 2 inches high. Stand with your toes upon the board, and your heels resting on the floor. Lean forward a trifle and lift both heels off the floor as high as you can. You are now balancing on your toes and balls of your feet.

1. Ready to Push   2. Explosive Push

PUSH THE WALL! Sit on the floor facing a wall as close as you can. Place both feet against the wall about 3 inches above the floor. Bend knees, lean forward, and place both hands on the floor directly behind you.

On the signal, "Push the wall!" release your hands from the floor and with an explosive push with your feet see how far you can slide away from the wall. Do this exercise on a linoleum or smooth wooden floor.

Leg Shot Put.　Tie a 10-pound bundle of magazines or newspapers together. Lie on your back and place the bundle upon your feet. Get set to straighten your legs slowly upward and forward, and with an explosive leg push, fling the weight as far as you can.

Play this game with your friends and see who can "put the shot" the greatest distance. This exercise should be done outdoors or in a gymnasium.

1. Balance the Weight

2. Explosive Shot Put

What's Your Speed?

Watch the way a quick-moving player steals a base, how a swift basketball forward blocks an opponent's pass, how a speedy sprinter moves like the wind! Most sports and games call for quick moves. You can improve your speed by practicing these exercises.

1. Pretend you are an outfielder. As the pitcher lets go and at the moment the ball meets the bat, sprint quickly for that fly ball coming toward you. Make the catch before the ball touches the ground.
2. Here comes a high fast ball. Make a quick turn, look over your shoulder, keep your eyes on the ball, sprint with it, and make the catch.
3. Work to catch the different passes in football that are just out of reach.
4. Imagine you are guarding a nimble-footed basketball opponent. He gets away and moves toward your right; left; behind you, and straight ahead. Dash quickly into position and guard him wherever he goes.

There are many more speed drills you can try. Sprint for those tennis balls, volleyballs, and badminton birds. See if you can make up some speed drills of your own.

50-YARD DASH! On your mark! Place the thumbs and first finger of each hand just behind the starting line. Place the toes of your left foot about 12 inches behind the starting line and the right foot about 12 inches behind the left foot. Bend your knees and straighten arms with your hips a trifle lower than your shoulders.

Get set! Raise your hips to shoulder-height and lean a bit forward with the weight evenly divided on your hands and front foot. Look straight ahead.

Go! Push off hard with the forward leg, take a short step forward with the rear leg, continue to lean forward, pump with your arms, and run about 10 or 15 yards in this low-body position. Then straighten up slowly as you run across the 50-yard finish line!

For left-footed runners, place the right foot close to the starting line with the left foot behind it.

QUICK STARTS. The quick take-off is very important in almost every active sport or game. Practice the right way to make the quick start to improve your speed.

1. Take a comfortable standing position. On the word, "Go!" lean a bit forward, take a short step forward, and run with a burst of speed for 10 yards—using short, choppy steps.
2. Take the same starting position. Make a quick quarter-turn to the right and run hard for 10 yards.
3. Make a quarter-turn left and go!
4. Make a quick half-turn and run toward the rear.

SPEED UP WITH POWER! If you are healthy, you have plenty of built-in speed in your body. Hold on to the speed you have by being active, but try to add to your speed even if you add only a trifle more.

To build up more speed with power be sure to include one or two explosive power and speed drills with your regular workout every day.

CHAPTER 6

Increase Your Staying Power

Do you "huff and puff" when you climb stairs? Do you run out of "steam" long before a game is over? How long does it take you to breathe normally again after a heavy workout? Perhaps you need better heart and breathing endurance.

Stamina and Endurance

Space doctors tell us that the astronauts are "hale, hearty and healthy." They have well-conditioned bodies. Their hearts are strong. They can take much stress. They have great endurance and staying power for the job of exploring the world of space. Athletes also need this staying power or they would never be able to finish a game.

Active Breathing Machinery

If you want to be able to get plenty of work done, or play all through a game, your heart and lungs should be "tuned up." You burn up more fuel and use more oxygen when you are active in a game.

As you work and play, your body supplies food and oxygen to every muscle. When you keep active your heart, muscles, and food-supply system improve.

What Extra Stamina Can Do For You

Would you like to know exactly what a healthy heart and breathing system can do for you?
1. Carry more fuel and oxygen to the muscles so they can grow bigger and stronger.
2. Get rid of waste products from the muscles to make room for fresh fuel and oxygen.
3. Increase the number of red blood corpuscles that carry extra oxygen to the muscles.
4. Build a bigger lung capacity in which to store the oxygen that supplies the blood.
5. Keep you from getting tired too quickly.
6. Help you recover more quickly after hard work or a long, drawn-out game.

A Rule for Extra Stamina

Champion athletes and astronauts know how to train. They discipline themselves to obey health rules and the rule that heads the list is, *"No Smoking!"*

What Happens When You Smoke?

Smoking does *not* strengthen the body. It does *not* help the bones and muscles to grow. It does *not* increase speed or endurance. Smoking does *not* improve staying power.

72

Do you know what smoking *does* do? It raises the blood pressure and quickens the pulse. It speeds up the heart and affects the breathing system. It causes shortness of breath.

Smoking irritates the throat and lungs and can cause a lifetime of coughing. It interferes with good eating habits and can affect the digestive system.

And did you know that all smokers suffer to some extent from carbon monoxide poisoning? Can you imagine what effect all this may have on your staying power? Medical people, from your family doctor and your government, are warning everyone about the dangers of smoking.

For all these reasons and many more, you can see that growing boys and girls should not smoke for it is unhealthy and dangerous to the body. It is no wonder that coaches forbid smoking for young people who wish to try out for athletics.

Remember this Rule!

Smoking is not a need. It is a habit that is easy to get into and hard to break. So, do not allow yourself to get into this habit.

Stamina Drills

Check with your doctor. If you have a good healthy heart, try these exercises and see the amount of endurance you have at this time. Then work at them a little at a time, every day, to improve your stamina.

1. Running
Run in place as fast as you can for ten seconds. Use low and high knee action and pump your arms vigorously. Rest for ten seconds. Repeat five times.

2. Stool Step-up

Stand close to a stool or bench which is from 12 to 20 inches high. Place right foot on the stool. Then step up with your left foot. Quickly step down with the right foot and then with the left foot. See how many times you can do this exercise in one minute. Rest for one minute. Repeat this one-minute exercise three times with one-minute rest periods between each.

3. One-Foot Step-up

Place your right foot squarely upon the stool and keep it there all through this exercise.

On the word, "Go!" bring your left foot up on the stool. Then step down with the left foot. See how many times you can step up and down with the left foot in one minute. Come up to a complete stand each time both feet are on the stool.

Rest for one minute. Repeat this exercise for three one-minute periods. Then practice with your right foot.

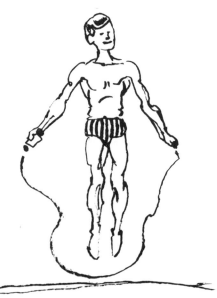

For More Endurance

4. Rope Jumping

Jump rope for one minute without stopping. If you miss a skip, just keep going. Rest for fifteen seconds. Do three one-minute jumps with a fifteen-second rest period between each jump workout.

CHECK YOURSELF. Were you able to do each exercise without fighting for air? Did your muscles become tired? Did it take very long for you to recover and begin to breathe normally again?

If you had no trouble, do these drills a greater number of times and work at a faster pace. If the drills made you feel tired, don't be discouraged. Try them with a longer rest period between each set of drills. Or do the drills fewer times.

Don't rush! Here are some exercises that will help to improve your stamina gradually.

Walk and Run

1. Run at full speed for 50 yards. Walk briskly for 15 yards. Repeat this walk-and-run exercise three times without stopping.
2. Trot at an even pace for 200 yards. Do not try to run as fast as you can. Just run at an even pace. If you can do this without getting tired, increase the distance to 300 or 400 yards.
3. Trot for 100 yards. Walk 25 yards. Repeat this trot-and-walk five times without stopping.

    If these exercises are hard to do, try them at a slower pace or shorten the distance. Keep working and you will improve your endurance.

Sports Stamina Drills

There are many movements in sports that can be used as drills to help build more staying power. You can condition your heart and breathing system by hiking, bicycling, and roller and ice skating.

Try one or more of these: touch football, soccer, basketball, running the bases in baseball. You can also work at hockey, swimming, and tennis.

Practice these exercises and sports drills regularly, day after day. End the practice drills with the feeling that you could have kept going a little longer.

Building Stamina

Everyday "Must" Exercises

1. Walk or bicycle to school (if there is a safe route and the distance is not too far).
2. Walk or trot around the block.
3. Walk or ride your bicycle to the store.
4. Help with heavy chores around the house. Carry out garbage, shovel snow, rake leaves, clean the garage, and ask your parents for other things to do.
5. Take part in school games and sports.
6. Join a neighborhood team.

Now, get to work and improve your staying power. What a good feeling it is to get a job done or stay and play all through a game.

CHAPTER *7*

Keeping Fit at Home

Would you like to have a "built-in" gymnasium in your own home? And a playground, too?

This fitness equipment can be yours with a little planning and some work. It may not be a complete or large gymnasium, but it will be a workable place and ready to use in your spare time.

Spare Time

You go to school. After school there is homework. Then what do you do? Sit and watch TV? Sit and listen to records? Sit and watch movies? Sit and snack?

All this "sitting time" you can use to be active and help yourself keep physically fit. Don't let that sitting time make you soft and flabby!

Spare Spaces around the House

Make use of that spare space around the house, both inside and out-of-doors. These spaces can be used for your fitness program. No doubt you can check off some areas like these: *Indoors:* basement, family room, game room, garage. *Out-of-doors:* carport, driveway, breezeway, patio, back or front yard, sidewalk along the side of the house.

Fitness without Equipment

Wall pulleys, rowing machines, and machine-made exercisers are big expensive pieces of equipment. You may buy these if you wish, but there are other ways to keep fit without this expensive equipment. In fact, there are many exercises and games that need no equipment at all.

The whole family can enjoy a fast game of tag. They can do stunts as forward and backward rolls. They can try cartwheels and hand-walks. Play touch football. Build pyramids. Do double somersaults. Wheelbarrow walk and hand-wrestling. Practice broad jumping. And it's fun to do setting-up exercises.

Also go on hikes, climb hills, and go swimming. So much fun and fitness with no equipment at all!

Fitness with Simple Equipment

There are many games you can play with very simple pieces of equipment. Here are some suggestions:

BALL GAMES. Do you like to shoot baskets? All you need is a basketball and a backboard and hoop. Fasten the backboard over a garage door or other handy place and try your skill.

If baseball is your game, get a bat and ball. Play "catch." Learn to run the bases. Practice pitching, fielding, and batting.

Backyard Basketball

For touch football and soccer, get the proper balls. Go outdoors and throw the football for accurate passes. Practice the different kicks.

Every member of your family, from the youngest to the oldest, can get into these ball games. The little ones can be the ball chasers.

MORE OUTDOOR FUN. For more fun with simple equipment get some roller skates. In the winter go ice-skating and sledding.

Put a wooden plug on your fishing rod and practice fly casting in your backyard. Or the whole family can get on bicycles, with fishing rods and a good lunch packed away on the carrier baskets, and head for a good spot. Try it!

HOMEMADE EQUIPMENT. There are also many kinds of equipment you can make for your home use. For example, do you get full use out of your bicycle?

BICYCLE EXERCISER.   Don't store your bicycle away when winter comes. You can ride your bicycle all the year round. All you have to do is build a stand and make a bicycle exerciser out of it. It's quite simple to do.

Year-round Bicycle Exerciser
(Indoor-Outdoor)

Use metal or wooden rods. Join the rods together firmly and make a stand. Place the hub of the rear wheel upon this stand so it is raised from the ground, and you have a bicycle exerciser. Now get into the seat, grasp the handlebars, and pedal away!

Make stands for your younger brothers and sisters and mount their tricycles so they will have exercisers, too.

Bicycle pedaling improves the heart and breathing system and develops strength and explosive power in the leg muscles. It's this explosive power that helps you jump higher and run faster.

LONG AND SHORT BARBELLS.   A good way to get rid of that flabbiness (if you have any) is to do workouts with barbells. And barbells are easy to make. All you need is a broomstick or metal rod, two empty *quart-size* cans (food cans are fine), and some cement.

Cut the broomstick or rod to a length of 4 feet. Pour cement into one empty quart can. Place one end of the rod squarely into it and let the cement dry. Then pour cement into the second quart can, place the other end of the rod into it, and let dry. You now have a long barbell.

To make a short barbell, cut a rod to a length of 1½ feet. Set both ends of the rod, one at a time, into *pint-sized* cans filled with cement.

Now exercise with the weights, and the muscles of your wrists, arms, shoulders, chest, and upper arms will become firm and strong.

Arm and Wrist Developers. What a powerful arm and wrist it takes to throw a ball from the outfield to the plate!

To make a wrist developer, shorten a broomstick to a length of 1 foot. Put a nail or drill a hole at the center. Tie a 2- to 5-pound weight with some strong cord through the hole so that the weight hangs about 3 feet below the rod. That's all there is to it.

Now grasp the rod with both hands, raise the arms to shoulder-height, and roll and unroll the weight. There is a well-known golf champion who carries one of these wrist developers in his traveling bag wherever he goes!

Grip and Wrist Developer. You can strengthen your handgrip and wrists with just a small rubber or sponge ball. All you have to do is squeeze the ball over and over again with each hand.

Or you may buy a wrist developer which is made of a spring inserted between two wooden handles. Squeeze the handles and develop your grip and wrists.

Horizontal Bar. Get on a horizontal bar and improve your wrists, arms, shoulders, upper back and chest muscles.

You can have a horizontal bar either inside or outside the house. Use a solid rod of steel from 1 to 1½ inches thick and from 3 to 6 feet long. Fasten it inside a doorway or to a beam in the basement or garage. Fasten the bar at a height of 6 to 12 inches above your standing reach for chinning and swinging exercises, 3 feet above the ground for bar and floor exercises.

For an outdoor horizontal bar get two solid 4- by 4-inch beams and set each one in a cement base. Then fasten the bar upon the beams.

Use the horizontal bar for chinning, hand-traveling, and many other exercises.

1. Climb up

Climbing Rope. Your whole body works when you pull on the muscles as you climb. Rope climbing is a fine, all-round body developer. It also improves the armgrip and arm and shoulder muscles.

For indoor climbing, fasten a rope to a beam in the basement or garage. Have your father check the beam for strength. Or tie the rope to a strong tree limb outdoors.

You don't need a long rope. Use a rope about $1\frac{1}{2}$ inches thick and from 6 to 10 feet long. Now get close to the rope, lie down, and pull yourself up to a sitting position and then to a standing position. Climb to the top with or without the use of your legs.

As you do the rope climbing, stretch those pulling muscles in your upper body. This is real exercise!

1. Arms only   2. Double rope stunts

ROPE CLIMBING

Tug-of-War Exerciser. Use a strong rope about an inch thick and from 6 to 10 feet long. Fasten one end about 4 feet above the ground to a wall or beam in the basement or garage. Or to a strong post or tree outdoors.

Dig in and pull on the rope and feel the muscles at work in your arms, upper body, and legs.

SHOT-PUT. To make a shot-put, fold some newspapers or magazines, one on top of the other, into a compact pile for a weight of 5 to 10 pounds. Tie the bundle firmly with strong rope and your shot-put is ready.

Then go outside to the driveway or backyard. Place the shot-put flatly upon the palm of your hand, hold it close to your ear, and fling the weight as far as you can. This is good explosive action for throwing, batting, and passing.

SPEED PUNCHING BAG. Some punching bags have a lightweight frame that can be installed into a wall or ceiling. Or you can buy a punching bag and swivel and make a rack for it. Fasten the swivel on the rack and you're ready to go.

Punch the Bag

Put on the gloves and punch away for better coordination, timing, and accuracy.

BALANCE BEAMS. There's no need to be "top-heavy" and awkward. Build a balance beam and learn to move with strength and control.

To make a balance beam, use a 2- by 4-inch board from 6 to 10 feet long. With the 4-inch side facing up, fasten both ends to a block of wood at each end about 12 to 14 inches above the ground.

Try the forward walk, backward, and sideward. Do other simple stunts such as walking on hands and feet (all fours) and leg raising on the board.

BENCH AND SAWHORSE EXERCISERS. A bench and sawhorse are handy pieces of equipment, for there are many exercises you can do with each.

To make a bench, use a piece of lumber about 6 feet long and 6 to 12 inches wide. Attach side pieces about 24 to 36 inches high at each end.

A sawhorse exerciser is made the same way as a regular carpenter's sawhorse, only it should be heavier and stronger.

On the bench and sawhorse you can do floor chin-ups, sit-ups, and push-ups. Or use it as a balance beam and do leg raising and other stunts.

BROAD JUMPING. For standing broad jumps indoors, all you need is a mat or some other soft padding to use as a landing place. When outdoors, just draw a take-off line and use it to test the explosive power in your legs.

Baseball and Football Fun

Paint two circles, one inside of the other, on a piece of old rug, canvas, or other strong material. Attach this target in the basement or garage about 1 foot away from a wall. Or outdoors, 1 foot away from a fence.

With a smooth motion, pitch the baseball at the bull's-eye. Also use a football, and practice passing right into the target.

"Tune-up" Golf

Golf is a game you can play all through life. So start your golf game now and enjoy it for a long time. Begin with short shots.

All you need is a good-sized cardboard box. Cut a hole about 4 to 6 inches in diameter in the middle. Place a weight on the inside of the box to hold it down. Then tilt it against a wall with a wedge to keep it steady.

Now chip that ball into the hole! This is good practice for short shots. You can also take this box outdoors and work on the short shots. *Never* practice golf on the rugs in your house!

For your putting game, dig a small round hole outdoors and place a small-sized empty food can into it level with the ground. Or you can buy a "putting cup" for indoor or outdoor practice.

To practice the full-swing shots, paint a target on some canvas or a rug and use it as a backstop. Some netting attached to each side helps to keep the ball within the target cage. Fasten this backstop to a tree or post a foot away from a garden wall.

As you begin your golf practice it is wise to use plastic golf balls.

ARM AND CHEST EXPANSION EXERCISERS. There are two kinds of expansion exercisers. One is made of steel springs with wooden handles that can be set to different strength positions. The other is made of solid rubber that remains in one position.

For a good workout, all you have to do is grasp a handle in each hand and pull hard. See your chest, arm, and shoulder muscles grow.

PORTABLE GYM SETS. If you decide to buy a big piece of equipment, a portable gym set is something the whole family can enjoy. There are many kinds of gym sets that can be used both indoors and outdoors.

They come in different sizes and are made up of many parts that can be added from time to time. A handy feature is that these sets are easy to set up or to take down and store away.

You can do chinning, ladder hand-walking, arm and shoulder dips, climbing, and many kinds of acrobatic stunts on these sets. Any number of people from one to a dozen can work out on a set at the same time.

The exercises are fun to do and are also fine for stretching, bending, pulling, and all-round pleasure.

Your Home Playground

Spend some time beforehand and plan your home playground. Check with the other members of your family to decide on the best location. Mark the spaces and set up equipment so you can start playing or exercising without any waste of time.

1. SHUFFLEBOARD. This popular game can be played indoors on a basement floor or outside your house.

Just paint the lines and numbers in the driveway in front of the garage, or on the sidewalk along the side of the house, or in some other handy spot. Then any time you want to play, the court is marked and ready.

2. BADMINTON OR VOLLEYBALL. Place two poles, the proper distance apart, in the backyard. Tie a net at

the right height and you are always ready for an exciting game of badminton or volleyball. If you don't have a net, use a lightweight rope.

Lower the net and you are set for a game of deck tennis, which is played with a small hoop. Also you can tie a tetherball to the top of one of the posts and you're ready for this game, too.

3. HORSESHOES. A long, narrow soft space near the fence in the backyard is just right for a game of horseshoes. Use removable stakes which can be put in place quickly and easily. Or get a rubber horseshoe set that you can use for your indoor game, too. You will enjoy playing horseshoes as you toss toward the target for those "ringers."

4. FOLLOW-THE-LEADER OBSTACLE COURSE. Get the whole family together for some obstacle running. Place boxes, stools, benches, and old tires on the ground at different places in the yard. Set up a few posts and crossbars here and there, and your course is ready.

Everyone, from the youngest to the oldest, can follow the leader. Run across, jump over, crawl under, walk through, and skip around the obstacles until the whole course is covered. This is vigorous fun!

MORE IDEAS. There are many more ideas for outdoor fun. Play hopscotch! Jump rope! Shoot marbles! Fly kites!

Invite your friends and neighbors to join in. You and your family and friends will put more "life" into your living. Best of all, you will have fun as you keep fit at home.

CHAPTER 8

Keep Fit Through Sports

Did you ever wonder why some people grow up to be champions in one sport and others choose another sport? How did they choose their particular sport? When did they discover that they had talent for it? This all began when they were quite young.

At one time these big-leaguers were young, just your age. They kept busy. They played games, went on hikes, swam, and ran races. While they were practicing and playing, they were also getting plenty of calisthenics at the same time. They were keeping their bodies healthy and strong.

These future champions were learning many new skills that were to help them enjoy their favorite sports later on, as they grew older. Perhaps this early training helped some of them make the team in high school or possibly the Olympic team!

What Is Your Favorite Sport?

Probably there is one sport you like best. Or there may be several you enjoy playing. It's not necessary to choose a favorite at this time. Right now it is important that you take part in games and get plenty of exercise.

As you play, you will discover that you have more skill for certain games than for others. You may even discover talent you never knew you had. This is the way the body grows as it works. Your interest in some special sport will depend upon your liking for it.

1. You may have a natural ability in this particular sport.
2. You may be the right size and have the needed strength for it.
3. You may be getting more out of this game because you feel that it is helping you grow bigger and stronger.

Remember this fact: No matter what your skills or favorite sport may be, try to learn several games that are meant for your age. This is not only a good way to learn about other sports; you will make new friends, too. As you play the game and join a team, the time will come when you will play in a big game.

Training for the Big Game

You may know how to shoot a basket, bat a ball, or kick a goal, but are you ready to play in a big game? Have you conditioned your heart, lungs, and muscles to use your sports skills in a hard, long-drawn-out game? All athletes know they must train to make the team.

The team doctor will not permit a player who is not in good physical condition to take part in a regular game. Athletes who have not trained and conditioned their bodies may not only injure themselves but they may hurt the team, too.

If you are "soft" and not in condition, you should not try to keep pace in a game with players who have trained their bodies and who play often in vigorous games. You must get your body in shape before a big game.

Put this important fact in your Fitness Notebook: "All the calisthenics, training, and sports exercise drills you use to prepare for an athletic contest help to improve the muscles and organs in your body just as much as when you play in the game."

Training for Sports

Coaches, trainers, and doctors watch their athletes carefully. They are examined and tested and checked. They must eat the right foods and get a proper amount of rest and relaxation. And they continue to do their sports drills and daily conditioning exercises. It is no wonder these champions are in good physical condition.

But body fitness for one sport may not be the kind needed for another sport. A powerful baseball pitcher may not have the conditioning needed for a hard game of football. The football player may not be ready for a fast game of basketball. Since all these players are in top physical condition, why is this so?

Different *sets of muscles* have to be more highly trained for some games than for others.

For example:

Baseball players spend a great deal of time developing their batting muscles.

Football players concentrate on conditioning their bodies to make tackles.

Basketball players sharpen their accuracy with a lot of basket shooting.

And the swimmer must train special pulling muscles to cut rapidly through the water.

So there are special drills to improve all players' ability in their particular sport.

But no matter what the sport may be, all players keep physically fit before, during, and even after the season ends. The warmups and calisthenics they do are good for all athletes.

Choose Your Special Workout

Do you get tired before your teammates do when playing a game? Do you play well during the early part of a game but find yourself slowing down before the game is over?

One reason you may tire easily in the game is that your heart and breathing system may not be in good condition. If this is the case, plan your training period to include drills that will improve your heart and breathing endurance.

If you don't do well in dodging, twisting, or pivoting, choose some drills that will improve your agility and flexibility.

If you are not sharp in passing, kicking, or shooting for baskets spend more time on speed and accuracy drills.

Perhaps you are a pretty fair infielder but weak as a hitter. This means that you should improve your shoulder, arm, and grip muscles. Pull-ups, push-ups, and weight-lifting exercises should help you.

Have you ever watched batters pick up two or three bats and swing them around their shoulders? This is what hitters do to improve their batting power. After several weeks of such training, you will find that the bat feels much lighter when you're up at the plate because you have developed your arm and shoulder muscles to swing with greater speed, timing, and power.

That's what the top athletes do. They work constantly to correct their weaknesses. The best thing is to keep at your special sports drills and calisthenics all through the year. However, work to improve your complete physical-fitness rating. Now let's find out about some special fitness skills that are needed for some of the more popular sports.

FOOTBALL AND SOCCER. In these games every player must be able to take body shocks and bumps. The backfield players in football and the forwards in soccer must have greater speed and agility than the other teammates.

Linemen must have extra strength and power in their legs to make forward charges. The ends should have nimble hands and the leg power to snare those passes. And the passer must have a good arm to send the ball and hit the bull's-eye.

All soccer players should have quick and nimble feet to control and make a foot dribble or kick the ball for a pass or goal.

Nimble Hands Catch Passes

Strength, Timing for Power Hitters

BASEBALL AND SOFTBALL. Every player on the team must have a good arm to make a strong throw and catch. The pitcher needs special throwing skills to control a curve-ball pitch. The catcher must have quick hands to be able to catch a fast ball after the batter misses the pitch.

Infielders are quick on their feet to stop hot grounders. And outfielders must cover a lot of ground to make a catch. The power hitters need good shoulder and arm strength with perfect timing to hit that long ball.

BASKETBALL AND VOLLEYBALL. All basketball players have coordination and accuracy to put the ball into the hoop. Some are "crack shots" with the two-hand stationary and jump shots and others seldom miss with the one-hand or lay-up shots.

The center and champion rebound players have explosive power in their legs. That's what gives them the speed to get control of the ball on the jump-off and rebounds. All the players should have agility and speed to pivot and fake and guard an opponent.

Volleyball players need power in their arms to serve the ball over the net. They must be able to set up a pass to a teammate without holding the ball. This means nimble fingers and good arm and hand control. They must have the skill and arm power to "spike," "smash," and "bat" the ball over the net.

TENNIS, BADMINTON, TABLE TENNIS. These sports all demand flexible joints for good shoulder and arm action. Tennis calls for fast foot movements to reach the ball and hit it over the net.

The great tennis players have tremendous explosive muscle power in the serving arm as they smash the ball over the net.

Badminton strokes are made with plenty of wrist action to get the shuttlecock (bird) over the net with speed.

Table tennis (Ping Pong) players must make lightning-quick movements with their hands to make accurate return hits. Players in all these fast-moving sports must practice for better timing in their strokes.

TRACK AND FIELD. The skills for track and field depend upon the event. For dashes you must have great speed and power in your legs. For the middle and long-distance run you need strength in leg muscles and a great amount of endurance in your heart and breathing system. The high jump and broad jump take great force and explosive power in the legs.

The pole vaulter has terrific pulling muscle force in the arms and shoulders. Shot-putters and discus-throwers work for perfect timing and explosive muscle power and force in the arms and shoulders.

TUMBLING AND GYMNASTICS. These sports call for many all-around physical fitness skills. Special skills are needed for some of these events.

Can you picture the perfect body balance and muscle strength of a gymnast who presses up to a handstand on the parallel bars? Or a tumbler who does a series of four back-flips in a row and ends up doing a one-and-one-half back body twist?

This means strong shoulder, arm, and abdominal strength. You also need fine body balance and control as well as flexibility in the hip and shoulder joints.

SWIMMING AND DIVING. Swimming is another sport that calls for all-around physical fitness training. You need speed in your arm strokes and leg kicks for the short races. For long-distance swims, you must have plenty of heart and breathing endurance.

All swimmers work for power in the pulling muscles of their arms and shoulders and the kicking muscles of their legs. Swimmers also need flexible hip joints and powerful abdominal and back muscles.

Divers must practice about the same skills as tumblers and trampoline performers to get perfect control and sense of balance when they are suspended in mid-air.

ICE-SKATING, ROLLER-SKATING, SKIING. You need body balance for all these sports. For ice-skating and skiing you must develop strength and power in ankle, knee, and leg muscles.

GOLF, ARCHERY, CROQUET. Timing and accuracy are important skills in all these target-hitting sports.

The golfer needs more coordination in his golf swing than the croquet player with his mallet. In golf, you must train for a strong armgrip and shoulder muscles to control the swing.

You need these same skills for archery. Also, it's important to keep the muscles absolutely still before releasing the bowstring.

BOWLING, HORSESHOES, SHUFFLEBOARD. You need to develop a good arm swing with control to hit the target when you play horseshoes and shuffleboard.

Bowling takes a somewhat stronger grip and arm-muscle strength to control the ball. A bowler must have good coordination as he moves forward to release the ball toward the target. This takes proper timing of the footsteps with the swinging of the arm.

HIKING AND BICYCLING. For long-distance hiking and bicycling, you need leg-muscle strength and heart and breathing endurance.

As you can see, some sports demand that players have more skill in one area of physical fitness than another. So, the wise thing is to condition your whole body. Then, no matter what sport you may choose, you'll be on your way. All you will then have to do is to spend more time in conditioning a certain area of your body to help you play better at the sport you like best.

That's how some young people grew up to be champions!

CHAPTER 9

A Special Word for Girls

Who is the most popular girl in your school? Who is your favorite among the women you know or read about? Is she a doctor, nurse, scientist, clothes-designer, teacher, or librarian? Is she a dancer, singer, writer, pianist, housewife, mother? Perhaps she is an Olympic champion!

What is the secret of her success? It's really no secret at all. No matter what her age may be, she is alive and alert. She may not be beautiful but she moves with poise. She glows with an interest in life. She is active! She gets things done. She is a person who is filled with energy and enthusiasm. She enjoys being alive!

The reason she is able to do things for herself and for others is that she is healthy. This feeling of *well-being* is something that did not happen all at once. Your favorite person began her road to success and good health when she was *your age*!

Look at Yourself!

Just take a good look at yourself. Do you slouch and shuffle when you walk? Do you sprawl when you sit down? How much of your time do you spend in sitting—

> at the telephone?
> in front of TV?
> at the movies?
> watching others play games?

Do you know what this slouching, sprawling, and sitting is doing to *you*?

Just think of all the bones, muscles, ligaments, and nerves in your body. Then add the heart, lungs, breathing system, and other organs. These organs and systems in your body need exercise!

Shape Up for Fitness!

No matter what her age may be, every young girl wants to be attractive. To have a trim figure. To walk with good posture and a graceful step. In other words, you want to look well and feel fit. You can—with some careful planning and a willingness to work at it. So shape up for fitness!

Do not loll around the house so much. Do not overeat. Do not make so many trips to the refrigerator and snack bar. Most important, start on your exercise program now!

Get Set!

Before beginning your fitness program, here are some ideas that may help you.

1. Do your exercises every day *at a certain time.*

Choose the most convenient time, either in the morning before school or later in the day or evening and *stick to that time every day!*

2. Wear comfortable clothes for your workouts. Shorts, bathing suit, or leotards. (Or pajamas early in the morning.) Work out in your bare feet or wear tennis shoes.

3. Get some exercise out of the things you do every day. When you go on errands, step lively and walk briskly. There's plenty of exercise in making beds, helping with the laundry, dusting, and other household duties.

4. When you carry books to and from school, shift the position of the books from one arm to the other.

5. Have some active fun on weekends.

   In winter you can go ice-skating, skiing, or tobogganing. When the weather permits, take long walks or go on hikes with your friends and clubmates. Ask your family to arrange some camping trips.

   Play baseball with your brothers and sisters. Go swimming. Practice tennis and golf strokes. Shoot baskets. Jump rope, play hopscotch and other games.

   These exercises and games will bend and stretch you into good physical shape! You will then be ready to enter your "teen" years with health, vigor, and pep!

Your Own Fitness Plan

You are the one who knows how you feel. You know when you feel well or when you are sick, when you feel tired, when you haven't the energy to do a single thing!

So before planning your program, understand what

physical fitness is and what it can do for you. Then visit your family doctor for a complete checkup.

Also, do some checking up yourself. You know whether you are tall or short, thin or flabby, overweight or underweight. Get out that tape measure and see how you measure up.

Your Measurements

Ask your mother, sister, or a friend to help you with these measurements. Then write them in your Fitness Notebook.
1. Height (Use a yardstick.)
2. Weight (Use accurate scales.)
3. Neck (Use a tape measure for the rest of the measurements.)
4. Upper arms
5. Chest
    a. Normal breathing
    b. Inhale for chest expansion
6. Waist
7. Hips
8. Thighs
    a. Lower
    b. Upper
9. Calves
10. Ankles

It's a good idea to take your measurements every two months. But if you have a weight problem (overweight or underweight) or if you get tired easily, measure yourself every month.

What's Your Fitness Rating?

The tests in Chapter 2 gave your physical fitness rating. The Kraus-Weber and Youth Fitness tests measured your fitness rating and also pointed out your weak spots.

When you know your weaknesses, be sure to choose exercises that will help you most. Practice the exercises in these tests and mark your scores in your Fitness Notebook. Then every three months take the tests again and watch your improvement.

In addition to working on the exercises in these tests you will find in other chapters many more exercises, games, and sports drills that girls can do. Practice as many of them as you can. They will help to give you more bounce and energy and that "look-alive" feeling!

For That Slim Neckline!

Does your head droop? Do you see a suggestion of a double chin? Hold that line and put a stop to something that will make you act and look older than you are. Get your *chin up* with these exercises.

CHIN BOUNCE. Stand comfortably with hands on hips, head up. Look in the mirror as you do this exercise.

Press your chin down as far as it will go. Now move it slowly to the right with short, bouncy, up-and-down movements until it reaches over the right shoulder. With the same bouncy movements, move your chin all the way over to the left shoulder. Relax and come back to the starting position.

STAR-GAZING. Bend your head back and stretch your chin upward as you do when you look up at the stars. Now, with head back and chin up, slowly move your head toward the right shoulder as far as you can and then toward the left shoulder. Stop and relax.

NECK CIRCLES. Bend your head forward. Move it toward the right and around toward the back and to the left and return to position. Your head has moved around in a complete circle. Make two circles slowly. Then make three more at a faster rate with zip and speed. Now do this exercise starting toward the left.

WALL HEAD CIRCLE. Wrap a towel around your head for this one. Stand 12 inches away from a wall with your back toward it. Press your head against the wall, keep arms at your sides, cross right foot over the left, and roll toward the left with your head against the wall. Keep rolling and cross the left foot behind the right until you have made a complete circle.

As you practice this head roll, keep your neck muscles tight and firm. This is an excellent neck conditioning exercise!

For more head and neck action do the head tug-of-war in Chapter Three. Try a fast game of volleyball, badminton, or dodge ball. Do the crawl stroke on dry land or in the water. Join your friends for some basket shooting.

For Firm Muscles

A girl does not look good with the same bulgy muscles that boys have. Flabby muscles do not make a girl attractive either. What you need are *firm* muscles.

It's the firm muscles in the upper arms and chest that help you walk with your head held high. You need firm muscles to walk with a spring in your step. To carry groceries and books. To do chores around the house.

In sports and games you need firm muscles to bat a ball, swing a tennis racket, and to swim. Firm muscles will not allow you to become "round-shouldered." So, let's begin with some exercises that will give firmness to your muscles.

WAKER-UPPER. This exercise will help you start the day with vigor! Stand in a comfortable position. Grasp one wrist with your knuckles facing you and raise both arms overhead.

Pull up hard on your wrist and reach for the sky! When both arms are stretched high, take a deep breath. Exhale and relax, keeping the arms overhead. Do this exercise six times: stretch high and inhale, relax and exhale. You can also do this exercise while sitting down or lying on your back.

WRIST PULL. Stand straight with arms behind your back and grasp one wrist. Pull down and outward with your arms so you can feel the stretch in your arms and chest. Pull the shoulders back and take a deep breath. Repeat six times: pull down and inhale, relax arms and exhale.

TABLE TUG-OF-WAR. You can do this one in school at your desk (when you are not busy) or at home. Place both hands down upon desk shoulder-width apart. Push hands down on the table or desk without raising your shoulders. Inhale as you push. Hold this position for three seconds. Exhale and relax. Repeat six times. This exercise can also be done in front of your dresser.

Arm Twister

a. Stand with feet a few inches apart, hands at your sides. Move your arms straight back past your hips, elbows straight. Twist arms in and out, five times.

b. Raise arms sideward, shoulder-high; twist your hands, palms up and twist again, palms around as far as they can go.

c. Stretch arms high overhead and twist the hands in and out again.

d. Bend forward at the hips, lower your arms, and twist hands in and out again.

Sitting Windmill. Sit on the floor, legs spread, and raise arms forward to shoulder level. Touch left toe with your right hand and stretch your left arm back. Repeat toward the opposite side. Do this one ten times in each direction.

And don't forget to do the shoulder shrugs and solo tug-of-war exercises in Chapter 3. Also do pull-ups, push-ups, and rope climbing.

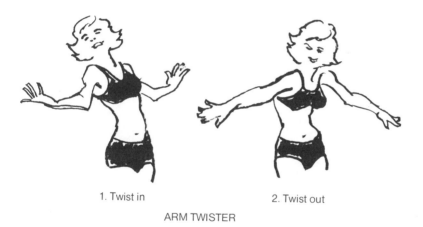

1. Twist in   2. Twist out

ARM TWISTER

Watch Your Waist!

Your waist and hips are two places that begin to take on weight quite quickly as you grow into your teens. Then you may become sluggish and slow-moving. When this happens you'll lose out on a lot of fun. So keep your body firm and attractive with these exercises.

Knee Hugs

a. Sit on the floor with your back close to a wall, sofa, or heavy chair. Bend your knees close to your body, wrap both arms around them, and press hard against your body. Relax. Repeat this knee-squeeze exercise five times.

b. Stand with your back against a wall. Raise one knee, wrap both arms around it, and press against your body. Now, with the other knee.

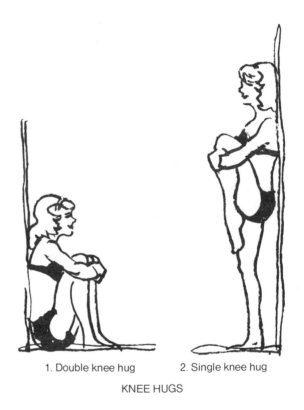

1. Double knee hug   2. Single knee hug

KNEE HUGS

WINDMILL "SLAP." Stand with feet spread wide apart. Raise arms forward to shoulder-height. Bend forward until your shoulders are hip-high. Twist at the hips, slap left ankle with your right hand, and whip the left hand up and back.

Without stopping, twist again and slap your right ankle with your left hand, whipping the right hand up and back. In this forward-bend position, slap each ankle, alternately, ten times.

RUBBER-BAND STRETCH. Stand with feet widespread. Raise right arm upward. Place your left hand against the left thigh. Look straight ahead and with short bobbing movements bend toward the left as far as you can and slide the left hand along the thigh. At the same time, reach over your head with the right arm as far as it will go. You should feel a stretch and pull along the whole right side.

Without stopping, raise up to the starting position and repeat this exercise toward the right side. Do this drill four times on each side.

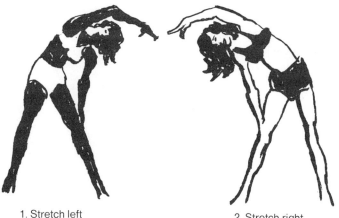

1. Stretch left   2. Stretch right

RUBBER-BAND STRETCH

Spin Around

a. Sit on the floor with feet together. Place both hands on the floor a trifle behind your body. Bend elbows just a bit and lean back just enough to put some weight on your hands. Raise legs, keep feet together, knees straight, and hold this position for five seconds.

b. From this position, spin around in one spot on the floor with the use of your hands. You may bend your knees a trifle if you wish.

More Waist Slimmers

Here are more waist slimmers you can add from time to time.

a. sit-ups
b. forward rolls
c. backward rolls
d. cartwheels
e. log-rolling (Lie on the floor, body straight, arms close to sides and roll over and over.)
f. hand-and-toe kick (Raise one hand shoulder-high and kick it with your foot.)
g. catching baseball grounders
h. swimming (In the water or dry-land practice.)
i. bowling (Step action.)

For More "Leg-Bounce"

When your legs get tired, the body begins to sag. And when that happens, your fine posture is gone and you get that "tired look." So put "bounce" in your legs. You'll walk with grace and poise. This alive, alert feeling will help you run, work, and play with vigor and vitality. Shun that tired look by exercising the legs, ankles, and feet.

FEET IN-AND-OUT. For firm thighs, calves and ankles.

Sit on the floor with feet shoulder-width apart, hands on the floor behind you. With straight knees, turn feet inward until the toes touch. Then turn your feet outward as far as you can. Repeat six times.

Foot Tug-of-War

1. Take the same position on the floor. Press both feet together. Slowly bend the knees and slide the feet closer toward your body until the soles of both feet are flat against each other. Push each foot against the other as hard as you can for five seconds. Keep on pushing as you slide your feet forward to the starting position. Relax.
2. Sit on the floor, cross one leg over the other, and hook your ankles tightly. Bend knees outward and pull with both legs for five seconds. This tug-of-war will stretch, trim, and strengthen your thighs and ankles.

LEG SCISSORS. Sit on the floor, hands behind you, legs straight. Cross left foot over the right as far as it can go. Without moving your hands from the floor, come back to the starting position. Do the same with the opposite foot. Do five times with each leg.

Leg Stretching

CHAIR STRETCH. Use a kitchen chair. Stand 12 inches away from the chair with hands on hips. Place one foot on the chair.

With shoulders back and head up, lean forward as far as you can over the knee that is on the chair. Keep the standing foot straight and rigid, with the heel flat on the floor. Repeat five times with each leg. You should feel a strong pull in the back of the standing leg.

BALLET POSE. Use a chair or dresser as a ballet bar. Stand with your left side nearest the chair, place your left hand on it, and your right hand on your hip.

Keep both legs straight, bend forward and raise the right leg backward until your shoulders and raised leg are level. Remove your hand from the chair and see if you can hold this ballet pose for five seconds. Turn around and try it with the other leg.

TOY SOLDIER. Keep arms and upper part of your body relaxed. Tense your hips, thighs, calves, and legs. Now walk twenty steps forward like a toy soldier with stiff knees. Turn around and walk twenty steps more.

CHEER LEADER ROCKET! With feet together and arms loose at your sides, take five short soft bounces up and down about 3 inches off the floor. On the sixth bounce push off hard, swing your arms high and shoot up like a rocket! Repeat the short bounces and rocket jump five times without stopping.

Always bounce on the ball of the foot and keep knees slightly bent.

FOR MORE BOUNCE! Try putting on your socks and shoes while standing on one foot. Rise up on your toes with elbows high as you comb your hair. Raise your arms and rise on your toes like a ballet dancer as you slip into your clothes. Bend down and keep knees straight as you tie the laces on your shoes.

Include at least three of these exercises in your daily fitness routine: jump rope, walk the balance beam, do the kangaroo and rabbit hops, practice heel-and-toe raising, ride your bicycle.

Another good leg exercise is picking up marbles with your toes. Also run short dashes. Swim. Play tennis, softball, volleyball, soccer, and badminton. The idea is to get on your feet for your share of games, exercises, fun, and fitness.

The popular girl weighs right, looks right, and walks right. So, play and exercise with vigor! Get on the Fitness Team for grace, poise, and glowing good health!

CHAPTER 10

Jogging—Walking—Hiking

What would happen if all the planes, trains, buses, and cars stopped? For a day? Or a week? Or longer?

Years ago, before the age of railroads and airplanes and automobiles, how *did* people get around? They walked! They used foot power to get from one place to another.

Early Pioneers

No doubt you have seen pictures of early American pioneers walking beside their covered wagons as they traveled west. Horses pulled the wagons but very often the men, women, and children walked.

They walked over hills and mountains, through forests and across prairies. Day after day, in storm, rain, wind, and snow, the settlers walked. They chopped down trees and blazed trails and kept going.

The pioneers had to have strong bodies and good breathing systems to endure such hardships. They had to have stamina!

As new ways of travel came into use people walked less and less. Their breathing and muscle systems became less strong. Often in an emergency they did not have the strength and stamina to do what needed to be done.

Young people and grownups learned that they had to be more active. They found out that the extra use of leg and heart muscles made them feel stronger and healthier.

Again, people are beginning to use foot power. Like the early pioneers, they are walking! More than that, men and women and boys and girls have discovered that walking, jogging, and hiking is fun!

Walking! Jogging! Hiking!

What are walking, jogging, and hiking?

What is the difference between each of these popular sports?

What is the right way to do them?

Walking is moving along on foot by taking steps. When you walk you *do not run.*

Keep the body in an upright position, chest up and head high. With knees and ankles limber, point the toes straight ahead. Push off with the rear foot as your front heel begins to land forward.

Move the legs directly forward from the hips, swing the arms and shoulders freely, and step along briskly. The walk can be slow or fast. If you really like to walk fast you may enter a walking contest in a track meet.

Jogging is a form of running. It is an easy, relaxed kind of run at a slow pace. There are several kinds of strides used in jogging.

Heel-to-Toe Jog

This is a popular jogging style and is used by the most people.

Land on the heel of the front foot with a springy forward movement of the body, push off on the ball of the foot, and keep going with an easy, bouncy step.

Practice this style until you can do it comfortably and easily.

Flat-Foot Jog

Step forward and land flat-footed on the entire bottom of the foot and keep going. You will really slap the ground with each step.

Every time your foot hits the ground you will feel a slight jar up and down the spine.

Ball-to-Heel Jog

Land on the ball of the front foot, quickly touch down with the heel, and push off for the next step. And keep jogging.

After some practice, choose the one jogging step that is most natural and comfortable for you.

A hike is a long walk. You may take a hike in a park, along a city street or boulevard, upon a country road, or through a trail in the woods. The hiker usually uses the heel-to-toe stride.

Your steps may change somewhat when you hike up or down a hill and your body will lean a bit forward or back as you adjust to the ground you are walking over. But mostly, try to walk in an upright position.

There are times when you may walk slower. Then again, you may walk faster to reach a certain place, like a camp, at a definite time.

So, step out briskly, head and chest up. Swing the arms freely forward and back in rhythm. Take your steps with a good upward-and-forward knee action. Breathe through the mouth and nose. Enjoy!

Your Walk-Jog-Hike IQ

How much should a person do? Can you tell when you've had enough? Do you know when to stop? You should make sure that you are healthy enough to jog, walk, and hike.

After a long walk, jog, or hike, how do you feel?
Do you tire easily?
Are your legs sore the next day?
You ought to know how far and how fast you may go without danger to your health. Walking, jogging, and hiking should not be a strain. You are not trying to break speed records. It should be a pleasant experience.

Remember: Before you start the walk-jog-hike program, be sure to have a health checkup by your family doctor. Then you will know how far and at what speed you may practice walking, jogging, and hiking.

For General Good Health

The President's Council on Physical Fitness and Sports has written books that tell why people should take part in jogging, walking, and hiking. There are many good reasons:
To improve the heart, lungs, and blood vessels.
To make the body muscles firm and strong.
To help build "staying power" or endurance.
In addition, it is a good way to improve posture, take off weight (if that's what you need), and help one look better and feel stronger, and it also gets people away from TV sets and into the outdoors.

Is baseball your favorite outdoor sport? Have you ever had the thrill of jogging around the bases after hitting the ball over the fence for a home run?

The walk-jog-hike program will help keep you in shape for that "jog-around-the-bases" and for other sports you like.

600-yard Run-Walk Test

To build up general good health, strength, and endurance try these tests.

The 600-yard run-walk is a good test to build up endurance (See Chapter 2, page 34). The idea of this test is to see if you have the stamina to cover 600 yards. You may run any portion of the 600 yards, or you can walk part of the way if you wish. Check your rating on the charts on page 34–35.

Plan your exercise according to the rating you made. If you scored well in this test, step right along and jog-walk-hike. If you did not do well, you must build up your strength and endurance.

Stool Step-up Test

The stool step-up will help build strength and endurance (See Chapter 6, pages 71–76). Stand close to a chair or stool around 15 inches high. Place the right foot upon the stool, step up with the left foot, and quickly step down with the right foot. Keep going! This should be a four-movement exercise. See if you can do it 30 times a minute for *two* minutes. Then sit down on the stool and rest for two minutes. If you get tired before the two minutes are up, *stop* and try this test for only *one* minute. Also try the test on page 123.

Do not rush! Work to strengthen the leg and body muscles. Improve your breathing system.

In Small Spaces

All through history and in recent wars, prisoners of war have kept alive and in fairly good physical condition because they kept moving. Many prisoners of war lived in small cells, cramped for space, but they thought of ways in which to move about.

One man told about the way he worked to keep fit. He felt compelled to exercise. He tried to jog in place for 7 miles. How do you think he was able to measure 7 miles as he jogged in place in his little cell?

This man kept his mind active as well as his body. To pass the time more quickly he did arithmetic problems in his head. He also worked out mathematical puzzles and games. He worked for *total fitness*. And he made it! He kept strong enough mentally and physically and was able to survive in good shape.

Don't forget the astronauts in spaceships. There is very little room in spaceships. On their long flights they do exercises to stay limber. Although they have the problem of weightlessness to overcome, they manage to do their exercises and to jog.

Where can *you* jog? Almost anywhere! In the parks and playgrounds, on the sidewalk, and in your own backyard. A regular track or gymnasium is always fine and so is the inside of your house. You can even jog in your own room.

Keep Moving!

Keep moving with a purpose. The idea is to exercise so that you will be strong and healthy. There are so many ways to keep moving. Alone in your room you can walk in place or jog in place. Start at a mild, slow pace. Then step up with high knee action and speed.

Make a list of ways in which you can be active:
1. Jog to the store for your mother and father.
2. Walk or jog as you run errands for neighbors.
3. Jog or walk outdoors with your dog. Or your neighbor's dog.

You can keep moving as you help others who need

help. Handicapped people, and those who are not well, all need to be as active as they can be.

There are boys and girls and grownups in wheelchairs who cannot walk. Arrange to take them outdoors at certain times. Walk briskly as you push their wheelchairs.

Walk with crippled children.

Walk or jog with children who are blind.

Can you think of more ways to keep moving and also help others? Remember: Always get permission and instructions when helping those who are handicapped.

Watch the Joggers

People who are well should keep active to stay well. That's what more and more people are learning to do. Early in the morning or after work you see them jog.

They huff and puff along streets and sidewalks, parks and highways. Doctors, lawyers, men and women, old and young. A mailman jogs from 3 to 10 miles every day after work. Members of the fire department jog as part of their exercise program. An office worker jogs from the railroad station to his office every morning.

Boys and girls jog, too. They jog as they warm up before a basketball game or track meet. They jog around the playground at school. They jog with their family and friends.

What to Wear

No special clothes are needed for these exercises. You don't need much equipment, either. Just wear comfortable clothes and shoes. The clothes should be loose enough to allow freedom of movement.

Socks should be soft, thick, and must fit properly. Shoes must be well-cushioned, comfortable, with soles that prevent slipping.

Dress lightly for warm weather and wear warmer clothes when the weather gets colder. A cap, ear protectors, and gloves are useful for cold weather. If you form a club you may wish to get uniforms.

Hiking Clubs

Hiking is fun! Especially when you hike with friends. Try a family hike. Join a hiking club. Or get together with your friends and form a hiking club of your own.

Get information about starting a club through your gym teacher, librarian, YMCA, CYO, or community center. Another way you can be sure of hiking is to join the Scouts. This means girls, too!

Warning Do not go out on a hike alone. Always talk over your hiking plans with your parents or guardians and be sure to get permission from them. Always try to have an adult along.

On the Hike

All set! Are you wearing comfortable clothes and shoes? How about a camera? You may want binoculars, too. Are you taking lunches along? What kind of hike will this one be?

Are you a fossil hunter? Perhaps you are lucky and live close enough to places where fossils may be found.

So you like to collect rocks? Certain kinds of rocks

are found in different parts of the country. Get books from the library and find out what kind of rocks are near where you live.

Walk along nature trails. How many trees and plants do you know? Can you recognize birds by their bird calls? What woodland animals can you see?

Hike to historic spots. Our country is filled with places where important events in history took place. Visit historic markers, beautiful monuments, statues, and museums. It's thrilling!

If you may happen to take some unusually good pictures, enter them in a photography exhibit. Or your school or community newspaper may sponsor a photography contest. Jogging, walking, and hiking not only lead you into the outdoors, but also into a world of fun and action.

Jog! Walk! Hike! Make it a lifelong habit.

CHAPTER 11

Everyone Can Try To Be Fit

This is a story of two men. One had polio when he was a boy. He could not play games with other boys of his age because of a disability. But the doctor ordered him to work on an exercise fitness program. After much hard work and exercise, this boy improved. At last he was able to take part in sports. And this boy who had had polio when he was young grew up and became a champion mile-runner on an Olympic team!

The other man developed polio when he was close to middle age. He had to use crutches for the rest of his life, but he was active. He worked at exercises every day. He was a powerful swimmer. He enjoyed fishing and boating. In this way he conditioned his body. Although this man was never cured completely, he became President of the United States!

More Success Stories

One of the greatest photographers in our country was a woman. She began to lose control of her muscles and found that she could not hold the camera firmly. With special treatments and exercises she improved her fitness skills and was a news photographer for a leading national magazine!

There was a coach who was never able to play a game of basketball in his life. But, through his fine coaching, his team won the state high school championship!

Many people who could not take part in active games when they were young grew up to become great swimmers, golfers, bowlers, tennis players. There are even blind wrestlers!

Whether you have very little movement or a fair amount—you can hold onto what you have, you can improve a little; you can improve a great deal.

Whether the improvement is a great deal or not very much, every little bit counts, and you have to work as hard as you possibly can at the job of keeping fit.

You Should Keep Fit

If you can't take part in many games and sports, don't be discouraged. The people in the success stories did not give up. They worked out a fitness program that helped them get better. You can do the same.

So, no matter what your ailment may be, there *are* exercises you can do. There are special exercises and contests for those who are underweight or overweight, for the blind and deaf and for those with weak feet or backs, and for boys and girls in wheelchairs. Most important, there are exercises and also contests for those who are mentally slow learners.

And, sometimes although there is nothing really wrong, persons just may not have fitness skills because they have not developed their strength, endurance, agility, or coordination. These are the people who cannot keep up with their friends and classmates.

If this is your trouble, there is no reason why you cannot improve your physical skills. If your weakness is just a lack of physical development, let's take a test and see where you stand.

TEST FOR PHYSICALLY UNDERDEVELOPED. In addition to the regular physical fitness test, the President's Council on Physical Fitness and Sports has worked out a special test to measure those who are *underdeveloped*. This test is made up of four simple exercises for both boys and girls.

It includes the Recovery Index Test, pull-ups, sit-ups, and squat thrusts. These exercises show if you are too physically underdeveloped to play and work with other boys and girls of your age. See Chapter 2 for instructions on how to do boys' and girls' pull-ups and boys' and girls' sit-ups. Then take this test and see how well you can do.

THE FOUR EXERCISES

1. *Recovery Index Test.* This will tell whether you have good heart and breathing endurance. Have someone time this test with a stopwatch or a watch having a second hand. Place a chair, stool, or platform 16 inches high directly in front of you. The height may change from 14 inches for shorter persons to 20 inches for taller youngsters.

INSTRUCTION FOR RECOVERY INDEX TEST

1. On signal "Up," start by placing *right foot* on stool.
2. Quickly step onto the stool with the *left foot.* (You now have both feet on stool.)
3. Immediately step down with the *right foot.*
4. Then down with *left foot.* This completes the "Up" (one), two, three, four rhythm count action. Make this "step-up-and-down" movement, *30 times a*

minute for four minutes. The signal "Up" comes every two seconds. After four minutes sit down and remain quiet for one minute.

TAKING YOUR PULSE RATE

Try to get help from a nurse, teacher, or parent when you're ready to have the pulse rate checked. Older youngsters can learn to work with a partner to take each other's pulse rate.

You can find the pulse by placing middle and index finger of one hand firmly to the inside of the wrist of the other hand, on the thumb side. Try it on yourself! Then try to locate the spot on someone else. Do you feel the pulse on the tip of your fingers? Now follow this plan to check your rating after completing the four-minute exercise.

1. After a *one minute* rest take the pulse rate for 30 seconds. Record the number of pulse counts.
2. *Two minutes* after the exercise check the pulse again for 30 seconds. Record the pulse counts.
3. Check the pulse again *three minutes* after the exercise for 30 seconds. Record the pulse counts.

SCORE FOR RECOVERY INDEX TEST

For all boys and girls. Total all three 30-second pulse counts. Find your recovery rating:

  total 199 or more is a rating of *Poor*
from 171 to 198 is a rating of *Fair*
from 150 to 170 is a rating of *Good*
from 133 to 149 is a rating of *Very Good*
from 132 or less is a rating of *Excellent*

If you failed to complete the four minute exercise or scored poorly on the test, *check with your doctor.*

2. *Pull-ups for Boys And Girls.* This exercise will measure your arm and shoulder strength. See Chapter 2 for instructions.

124

Score For Pull-ups. *Boys* age 10 to 13 should be able to do *one* pull-up. Age 14, *two* pull-ups. Age 15, *three* pull-ups. Age 16, *four* pull-ups. Age 17, *five* pull-ups. *All Girls* ages 10 to 17 should be able to hold the *Flexed Arm Hang Pull-up* for 3 seconds.

3. *Sit-ups for Boys and Girls.* This exercise will measure the strength in your stomach muscles and some flexibility in the hip joints.
   Score for Sit-ups. *Boys* age 10 should be able to do *twenty-five* sit-ups. Age 11, *twenty-six.* Age 12, *thirty.* Age 13, *thirty-eight.* Age 15, *forty-nine.* Age 16, *fifty.* Age 17, *forty-five.*
   Girls from age 10 to 14 should do *twenty-five* sit-ups. Age 15, *nineteen.* Age 16–17, *eighteen.*

4. *Squat Thrust for Boys and Girls.* This exercise will measure the agility of your body. Have someone time this test with a stopwatch or a watch having a second hand.
   Begin this test by standing with hands at your sides. On the word, "Go!" see how many complete squat thrusts you can do in ten seconds.

Squat Thrust

INSTRUCTIONS FOR THE SQUAT THRUST

1. Bend knees to a squat and place both hands on the floor directly in front of your body.
2. Shoot or "thrust" your legs clear back so your body is straight.

3. Come back to the squat position again.
4. Return to the standing position with hands at your sides. You have made one complete squat thrust. Start again and keep going. At the end of ten seconds the timer will yell, "Stop!"

SCORE FOR SQUAT THRUST

Boys from age 10 to 17 should do *four* squat thrusts in 10 seconds.

Girls from age 10 to 17 should do *three* squat thrusts in 10 seconds.

If You Did Not Pass

If you were able to pass these four tests, keep working at your conditioning program so that you may be able to pass the regular Youth Physical Fitness Test shown in Chapter 2.

But if you failed in some parts, don't get discouraged. It just means that you have work to do. First, try to locate your weakness. Didn't you have enough strength to do the pull-ups? Then, work at drills that will give you more shoulder and arm strength.

If you were not strong enough to do the sit-ups, practice some exercises to improve your stomach and hip strength. Also work on drills for better body agility. In addition, play with friends of your own age and ability. Try to do some chores around the house. Carry the groceries. Work in the garden. Do more walking. And join your family in your home fitness program.

Then take the test again every six weeks until you are able to pass. As soon as you can pass this test, you can begin to work on the exercises in the regular Youth Physical Fitness Test.

Your Own Physical Fitness Program

While all people, old and young, should do conditioning exercises every day, some people must work on special drills to help strengthen or correct certain weaknesses.

Before you set out on your physical fitness program, go to your doctor for a complete physical examination. He will explain to you and your parents what kind of exercises to do and the kind of games you may play. Of course, you should follow your doctor's advice.

If You Have a Mental or Physical Ailment

Have you had some sickness or injury that lessened the use of some part of your mind or body? If this is so, you must make up your mind that this is the way it must be either for a short time or for a long time. But one thing is certain. No matter how limited your movements may be, your mind and body need to be active in order to remain healthy.

You may not be able to make fine or big sweeping movements but if you can bend or move your hips, elbows, legs, ankles, and arms, *try and move them as far as your ailment will allow!* And make these body movements as often as you can.

If you are able to pick up a fairly heavy weight, do not spend your time lifting objects that are light in weight. The important thing to remember is that you must use your muscles as much as their strength allows in order to get full use out of them. Try to follow these rules:

1.   Work toward being able to take care of yourself as far as your mind and body will allow.
2.   Make as many movements as you can *under your own power.*

3. Work to develop the greatest amount of use of
   your muscles and joints.

Programs for the Physically Disabled

Don't let a physical ailment keep you from being
active. Thousands of disabled youngsters and adults
are active in sports.

There are programs for the physically handicapped
in bowling, archery, riflery, flycasting, basketball,
baseball, swimming, track and field, and many other
sports activities.

Look into the *National Wheelchair Athletic Association*, which has established rules for all wheelchair sports other than basketball. The game of wheelchair basketball is controlled by the *National
Wheelchair Basketball Association.*

Young boys and girls who are physically disabled
can take lessons or compete in the many special sports
and physical fitness events that are sponsored by these
organizations.

You also have the opportunity to earn a *Handicapped Athlete of the Year* award which is given every
year for outstanding performance.

There is also a special *Wheelchair Sports Hall of
Fame* organization. This is where the permanent records of National and World wheelchair champions are
kept. Persons making outstanding contributions to
these programs are also voted into the Hall of Fame.

Programs for the Mentally Slow

Did you know that there are active programs for
youngsters who are slow or retarded mentally? One
popular organization promoting sports programs for

the mentally disabled is the *Joseph P. Kennedy Jr. Foundation*. It is named after the brother of former President John F. Kennedy.

SPECIAL FITNESS AWARD. Mentally slow, retarded, or handicapped boys and girls from age 8 to 18 can qualify for one of the many awards offered by the Kennedy Foundation. Check with your school, club, parents' organization, camp, or playground instructor for information on how you can qualify for the different awards.

If you want extra competition, the Foundation sponsors a *Special Olympics* for the mentally slow. Boys and girls aged 8 years and over are eligible. You have a choice of taking part in track and field, swimming, gymnastics, basketball, volleyball, floor hockey, bowling, physical fitness, and many more events.

Whether you are physically handicapped or mentally slow, you have an opportunity to get active in your favorite program.

Who knows? With daily hard work and the good care of your doctor, you may discover fitness and sports skills you never knew you had. So work hard to strengthen your mind and body. Improve the strength of the weak ligaments and muscles. You may even start to use some muscles you have never used before!

Some Exercises to Improve the Use of Wrists and Hands

If your wrists and hands are weak, these exercises and sports will help you. Work at some of these simple drills every day and you will improve the use of your wrists and hands:
1. a. Try to clench each hand.
Open and close each hand about five times.

b. Open the hand and hold the fingers close together.
Try to spread the fingers wide apart five times.

2. a. Rest one arm on a table with the palm down. Clench the hand and bend the wrist toward the right and to the left.

   b. Raise the hand and rest your elbow on the table. With a clenched fist, bend the wrist up and down. Try to move your fist around in a circle. Repeat the whole exercise with the other hand.

3. Press your thumb against the little finger, then against the next finger until you have passed all four fingers with the thumb. Try this with the other hand.

4. a. Press your fist against the palm of your other hand.

   b. Press the fingers of one hand against the fingers of the other hand.

   c. Press your fingers against the top of a table, desk, or against a wall.

5. Grip a wooden rod or broomstick with both hands. Roll it over and over in your hands without letting it drop.

6. a. Squeeze a rubber or sponge ball over and over again with each hand.

   b. Punch a boxing speed bag with your wrists held straight and firm.

   c. Practice on the typewriter or piano.

Some sports skills that will help strengthen your wrists and hands are:

Throwing and catching a baseball.

Shooting baskets.

Dart and marble games.

Playing shuffleboard.

Gripping a badminton or tennis racket.

Rod and reel casting.

Also try miniature or regular bowling if your hand is strong enough.

Improve the Use of Elbows and Shoulders

These drills can help you get more strength in your elbows and shoulders.

1. Clench your hand. Bend and straighten the arm at the elbow.
2. Clasp your hands together, bend one elbow and rest it against your body. With the other hand, start a tug-of-war and see if you can force that bent elbow to straighten. Then try to bend it again.
3. a. Raise both arms forward and then upward.
   b. Lower the arms to the side at shoulder-level and make some 6-inch circles with the arms.
4. Lean against a wall and push away with your arms.
5. Lie on your stomach and push up with your hands.
6. Sit on floor and do some pull-ups on a low bar.
7. Hold a lightweight book or other object in each hand.
   a. Bend and straighten the elbows with this weight in each hand.

1. Arm tug-of-war   2. Arm circling   3. Tight fist—elbow bending

FOR MORE ARM, SHOULDER STRENGTH

   b. Raise and lower the arms holding the weights. Also try these sports skills: swimming strokes, throwing a ball, shooting baskets, swinging a bat, golf club or tennis racket, archery.

If there is a wall-pulley exerciser or rowing machine handy, use this equipment as often as you can.

Improve the Use of Neck Muscles

Do you find it hard to turn your head and look around? Does your head droop? These exercises should help you.
1. Lower your head forward and back.
2. a. Keep eyes forward and bend your head toward the right and to the left.
   b. Turn your head to the right and to the left.
   c. Move your head around in a circle.
3. a. Play tug-of-war with your head and hands. Push your head against your hands and your hands against your head.
   b. Place your hands behind your neck and play tug-of-war again.
   c. Try it with the hands against your forehead.
   d. Play tug-of-war with your hands against the right ear, against the left ear.
4. a. Stand facing a wall and push away with your forehead.
   b. Stand with your back against a wall and push away with the back of your head.

1. Head circles

2. Arm and head press

3. Head tug-of-war

FOR STRONGER NECK MUSCLES

132

5. a. Lie on the floor. Press against the floor with the back of your head and with your feet as if you were going to raise your body from the floor.

b. Lie on your stomach with a pillow under your head and push down with your head and feet.

Other drills you can do—

The head movements in swimming.

Balance a book on your head.

The head position in archery as you let go of the bowstring.

The head position in the batting stance.

Improve the Use of Stomach, Back, and Hips

If you do not have the full use of your hips, back, or stomach muscles, work on some of these drills:

1. See how many of the exercises you can do in the Kraus-Weber Test in Chapter 2. This test points out the weaknesses in the lower back and the flexibility of the hips.

2. If you do not have full use of your legs try this simple exercise. Sit on a bench or stool and hold onto the seat with your hands.

a. Lean forward keeping your head up. Then lean back.

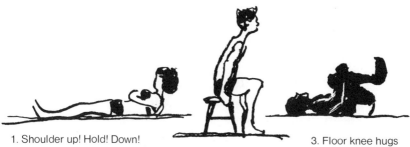

1. Shoulder up! Hold! Down!

2. Hip circling

3. Floor knee hugs

SOME BODY BUILDERS

b. Bend toward the right and to the left.

c. Try to circle around at the hips.

d. Raise your arms sideward to shoulder level and twist toward the right and to the left.

e. Also do all these exercises from a standing position if you can.

3. Get down on your hands and knees and crawl toward the right and then to the left. If you cannot crawl on your hands, try to crawl on elbows and knees.

4. a. Lie on your back with feet close together and arms across your chest. Raise your head and shoulders off the floor.

b. From the same lying position, bend your elbows and rest them on the floor near your body. Press down hard with elbows, and tense your whole body. Relax and try it again.

5. a. Lie face down and tense your whole body by stretching your legs, head, and arms. Relax.

b. From the same position on the floor or bed, try to form an arch by raising knees, head, shoulders, and arms from the floor. If this one is hard, help with your hands. Later, you may be able to do this one without using your hands.

6. Sit on the floor with your back resting against a wall. Bend your knees, wrap your arms around them and press close to your body. If you can't use your arms, just bend your knees and press against your body as hard as you can. You can also do this exercise while lying on your back or standing against a wall.

These drills should also be helpful—

Practice the follow-through in throwing, batting, and bowling.

The swing in golf and croquet.

The movements in swimming.

The rowing motion.

Improve the Use of Knees, Ankles, and Feet

If you do not have the full use of your legs you should do everything possible to strengthen them. Every tiny bit of improvement helps. Try to walk as much as you can. Also work on these exercises:

1. a. Sit in a chair and point your toes down as hard as you can.
    b. Point toes inward and outward.
2. Strengthen your ankles by moving your feet around and around in a circle, first with one foot, then with the other, and also with both feet at the same time.
3. See if you can pick up marbles or small stones with your toes.
4. a. Place your hands against a wall an arm's length away. Bend elbows, lean forward, and keep the feet flat on the floor.
    b. Place your toes on some magazines piled 2 inches high, and keep your heels on the floor. Press with the toes and raise the heels off the floor. This one will really stretch the back of the heels!
5. a. Sit on a chair with your feet flat on the floor. Raise your heels as though you were going to stand on your toes.
    b. Raise your toes as though you were going to stand on your heels.
6. a. Sit on a bed, sofa, or chair, with your legs down over the edge. Straighten your left knee until leg is straight. Then lower the leg. Repeat with the right leg. Now raise both legs together.
7. From a sitting or lying position, straighten your legs and tense them so they feel stiff.
8. Sit on a chair facing a table, the back of a sofa or bed frame and keep both feet flat on the floor. Raise yourself off the chair, keeping as much weight as possible on your feet.

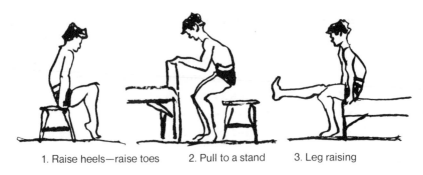

1. Raise heels—raise toes   2. Pull to a stand   3. Leg raising

SOME LEG EXERCISES

You can also try to kick a soccer or football. Catch fly balls and football punts and passes. Go bicycle riding and swimming and play basketball and volleyball if your legs are strong enough.

Of course there are always shuffleboard, archery, croquet, golf, and badminton. The idea is to *try and get on your legs whenever and as often as you can!*

More Fitness Drills

Were these drills easy for you? Then you can try many more in the other chapters. But easy does it. Work at these exercises a little at a time.

But if you are short on muscle strength, read Chapter 3 for exercises that will make your muscles stronger. Do you need more leg power? Read Chapter 5 for more power and speed. If you need body balance, agility, or coordination read Chapter 4 to help make your movements smooth and nimble. To strengthen the heart and breathing system read Chapter 6 to improve your staying power. Read Chapter 7 which tells about keeping fit at home. For additional family fun and outings read Chapter 7 and review Chapter 10 for fun in jogging, hiking, and walking. Then plan the program that is best for you.

Keep a record of your improvement in your Fitness Notebook. Write down—
The kind of exercise you are doing.
The number of times you do each one.
The amount of time you spend on each exercise.
Even if you can't do all the exercises in these chapters you will learn more about your body and how much it *can* do.

Fun at Camp!

It's fun to go to camp. Ask your parents to check with your doctor, school, YMCA, or church about camps for boys and girls who are limited in the use of their mind and body.

There are camps for the blind, hard of hearing, for boys and girls with heart ailments, for those in wheelchairs, and for those who are mentally slow or retarded.

You learn to make many things in the arts and crafts classes. There are nature-study hikes, swimming, boating, and many games. It's fun to gather around the campfire at night and sing songs, do stunts, and tell stories.

In addition to the fun, there are exercises and games that will help you become stronger so that you may be able to do more things. Some of these camps even allow the whole family to join in on the fun!

Things You Can Do

There are other ways of enjoying sports without taking an active part.

If you like football, basketball, track and field, or baseball there is no reason why you cannot help your team.
1. Be a team treasurer and take care of all the money.
2. Be a team secretary and keep a record of games.

137

3. Be a reporter and write up the game for your school or neighborhood newspaper.
4. Be a cheerleader or make up cheers, yells, and songs.
5. Be a maintenance person and take care of supplies and equipment. Mend articles that can be repaired.
6. Be a ticket seller.
7. Be a poster painter and make posters for games.
8. Be a scorekeeper or timekeeper.
9. Be a drillmaster and help the coach by helping the players in their workouts. (Check this activity with your doctor and get his permission to do this work.)

Baseball drills
    a. Toss the ball for batting or catching practice.
    b. Toss the ball so players may catch on the run.

Football drills
    a. Hold the ball in position for kicking practice.
    b. Make center snapbacks to ball-carriers who need practice in carrying the ball.

Basketball drills
    a. Toss the ball to players on the run who will shoot for baskets.
    b. Bounce pass the ball to players who need practice in dribbling toward the basket.

You can also make up some light drills of your own to help your teammates play a better game.

Best of all, it's always fun to go to games. If you can't go, watch the games on television or listen over the radio. Read sports books and magazines. And you can always help your team by being a loyal fan!

CHAPTER 12

Physical Fitness in the Future

Press a button inside your house. Listen! A power mower sets to work and mows the lawn while you sit in a comfortable chair and read a book.

It's almost time for dinner. Watch! A button is pressed and the meal is cooked! Press another button and the meal comes to the table on a tray upon wheels! Sounds fantastic, doesn't it? But these are some of the things being worked on in the field of automation to make life easier for everyone.

Right now there are automatic baseball-pitching and tennis-serving machines that toss balls so players can get all the practice they want. Already we are walking along on moving sidewalks, and calculators are helping you do long problems in arithmetic without your having to pick up a pencil!

While these new machines may make life easier, this also means that we will have more spare time on our hands and also that we will be using our bodies less and less. What will happen to our bodies if we don't use them? Do you remember?

1. The less you use your body, the less you will be able to use it for work or play.

2. The less you use your body, the more easily you may become sick.

3. The less you use your body, the less your muscles will do for you. In fact, you may lose the use of your muscles. When that happens you won't have the strength to pick up a baseball bat, throw or kick a ball, play games, or do any of the other things you like.

Age of Speed and Space

The man in the moon is no longer a fable. Before long you will probably take a trip to the moon! You will then be in a state of weightlessness.

Your body will have to be conditioned so that you can withstand a weightless state for a long time and still remain in a healthy condition. Space doctors and scientists are working on this problem of physical fitness now.

If you want to go to the moon just for the ride or as a worker, you will have to begin now to strengthen all the organs in your body to withstand the strains and stresses of living in the age of space!

Your Future Home Gym

With all the machines that are going to work for you and all the free time you will have, are you going to get caught as a *watcher* or will you be a *doer* and get in on the excitement of life in the age of speed and space?

While some ways of living will be different, many things will be the same as before. You will still need good muscle strength and endurance to play a musical instrument. You will still need muscle strength and endurance to play ball and to be a member of a team. Athletes will still have to develop muscle strength in the space age.

For these reasons and because we must all be strong

and healthy, here is what is going on in some of the new homes being planned.

Many homes are now being built with a regular physical exercise room which is equipped with soft mats, wall-pulley exercisers, weight-lifting sets, and other equipment to help keep the whole family in good physical condition.

We must keep this message in mind: The President of the United States wants all Americans to be strong now and in the future. As an American you can help your country as you help yourself to good health.

But, no matter how strong you may be, physical fitness is only one part of *complete fitness.*

To Have Complete Fitness!

In addition to fine physical fitness you also need these qualities to have *complete fitness.*
1. *Social Fitness*
   Do you get along well with others? Do you have consideration for other people? Do you respect and obey the rules and laws of your home, school, community, and country?
2. *Emotional Fitness*
   Do you act your age? Do you carry out duties and responsibilities without having to be reminded? Are you able to win or lose a game in a sportsman-like way?
3. *Intellectual Fitness*
   Are you curious to learn new things? Are you interested in the world around you? Do you enjoy reading?

If you can answer "Yes" to all of these questions and if you are able to meet all ten requirements for fine physical fitness, you are on your way to an enjoyable life.

Index